DHARDO RIMPOCHE

a celebration

DHARDO RIMPOCHE
a celebration

Edited by Sara Hagel

WINDHORSE PUBLICATIONS

Published by
Windhorse Publications
11 Park Road
Birmingham
B13 8AB

Printed by
Interprint Ltd
Marsa, Malta
Cover image © Clear Vision Trust Picture Archive
Design Vincent Stokes

British Library
Cataloguing in Publication Data:
A catalogue record for this book
is available from the British Library
ISBN 1 899579 26 5

Contents

vii   Illustrations

viii   Acknowledgements

1   Preface

FROM MEMBERS OF THE WESTERN BUDDHIST ORDER

7   Sangharakshita

9   Lokamitra

11   Nagabodhi

14   Kulananda

18   Malini

20   Vijayamala

23   Satyapala

27   Ratnaketu

31   Suvajra

34   Moksananda

40   Manjusvara

42   Gunabhadri

44   Sanghadevi

47   Chittadhara

49   Vessantara

52 Manjusvara

55 Sinhadevi

58 Maitreyi

61 Danavira

FROM KALIMPONG

67 Mahamati

69 Mr Jampel Kaldhen

75 Mrs N.C. Kaldhen

78 Mr Tashi Dorje

80 Mrs T. Wangdi

82 Mr Tenzing Amdo

83 Mr Dogah

88 Zenden Lhamo

90 Yankyidla

91 Tsering Wangdi

92 Jigmed Wangchug Kaldhen

THE MESSAGE OF DHARDO RIMPOCHE

97 Sangharakshita *on the first anniversary of Rimpoche's death*

109 Dhardo Rimpoche *The Flag*

112 Sangharakshita *Rejoicing in Merits*

114 Further Reading

Illustrations

ii   Photo by Kulamitra, courtesy Sunanda

6   Photo by Kulamitra, © Clear Vision Trust Picture Archive

26   *(top) Visit to Dhardo Rimpoche's home by Kulamitra, Kuladeva, and Ratnaketu,* © Clear Vision Trust Picture Archive

26   From Sangharakshita's collection, © Clear Vision Trust Picture Archive

54   Photo by Chittadhara, © Clear Vision Trust Picture Archive

64   From Sangharakshita's collection, © Clear Vision Trust Picture Archive

66   Photo by Kulamitra, © Clear Vision Trust Picture Archive

74   *(top) Mr and Mrs Kaldhen*, photo by Mahamati

74   *Mrs Kaldhen with Tenzin Legshad*, photo by Moksajyoti, © Clear Vision Trust Picture Archive

87   From Sangharakshita's collection, © Clear Vision Trust Picture Archive

94   From Sangharakshita's collection, © Clear Vision Trust Picture Archive

96   Photo by Kulamitra, © Clear Vision Trust Picture Archive

100   *Inside the ITBCI School*, from Sangharakshita's collection, © Clear Vision Trust Picture Archive

100   *(top) Morning assembly in the ITBCI School playground*, photo by Mahamati

105   Sangharakshita with Dhardo Rimpoche, 1967, © Clear Vision Picture Trust Archive

108   Illustration taken from the ITBCI School Report, 1963, courtesy Suvajra

Acknowledgements

Many people helped to make this celebration possible but particular thanks go to all the contributors, especially Mahamati, who collected the interviews from Kalimpong, and to all those in that far-away town with whom we are inextricably linked. Many thanks also to Dharmashura for the original idea, to Padmavajri and Moksajyoti for their research into photographs, and Shantavira and Dhivati for their careful checking.

Cherish the Doctrine
Live united
Radiate love

Preface

This book is a celebration of the life and work of the Tibetan Buddhist monk, Thubten Lhundup Legsang, better known as Dhardo Rimpoche. Dhardo Rimpoche died on 24 March 1990, at the age of seventy-three. This publication marks the tenth anniversary of his death – and rejoices in his life.

'Dhardo' is a contraction of Dhartsendo, the town in eastern Tibet where he was born, and 'Rimpoche' means 'Greatly Precious One', an honorific title given to lamas. As a boy, Dhardo Rimpoche was recognized as the incarnation, or *tulku*, of the chief abbot of the famous Drepung Monastery in central Tibet, the thirteenth in his line. However, though a high-ranking Tibetan lama of the Gelug School, Dhardo Rimpoche spent the greater part of his life in an obscure border town in northern India, running a small school for Tibetan refugee children, a school dedicated to preserving the culture, language, and religion of Tibet.

It might at first seem strange that the tenth death anniversary of this little-known Tibetan lama, even if a high-ranking incarnate lama, should merit a book; a book published, moreover, in the West. Dhardo Rimpoche never travelled to the West, he didn't set out to accumulate disciples, nor did he give famous, recorded teachings. Why, it might be asked, are we celebrating his life or commemorating his death? An extract from the preface to *The Wheel and the Diamond*, a biography of Dhardo Rimpoche, gives part of the picture:

> Dhardo Rimpoche was raised and educated within the classical Tibetan monastic
> system, but in 1949 he left Tibet to become abbot of the Tibetan monastery at Bodh
> Gaya. Then, for forty years, he lived in Kalimpong, in northern India, where he founded

an orphanage and school for Tibetan refugees and was the abbot of a local monastery. While there, he met and befriended an English-born Buddhist monk, Sangharakshita. The two men had been brought up in entirely different cultures; they differed in age and nationality, and they had been ordained into different strands of the Buddhist tradition. But their friendship was to influence many of the people, both Eastern and Western, who surrounded them.

Sangharakshita returned to the West, and in 1967 founded his own Buddhist movement: the Friends of the Western Buddhist Order (FWBO).*

The friendship between the two men was to have far-reaching consequences. The now worldwide Buddhist movement, the FWBO (or TBMSG as it is known in India), honours Dhardo Rimpoche as one of eight key teachers of its founder, Sangharakshita. In the 1980s many members of the FWBO travelled to Kalimpong to meet Rimpoche, inspired by gratitude for his teaching and respect for his practice. Back in the UK the visitors were motivated to raise funds for the continuation of Dhardo Rimpoche's work through the school he had founded – the Indo-Tibet Buddhist Cultural Institute (ITBCI) School. They brought gifts, asked questions, witnessed his work at the school, recorded interviews – and in return were showered by Rimpoche's soon legendary generosity, receiving gifts, hours of discussion and teachings, and always his wholehearted attention. He often said that he made no distinction between his own disciples and those of Sangharakshita.

Another reason we are publishing this book is simply that Dhardo Rimpoche's life is worthy of record, worthy of praise, and worthy of emulation. Rimpoche spent many hours every day in meditation and devotional practice. He used to say that, when young, he had not *felt* like a great lama but he had tried to *act* like one by developing wisdom and compassion, and so, over the course of time, he had *become* a Rimpoche.

* Suvajra, *The Wheel and the Diamond*, Windhorse, Glasgow 1991

He would urge his visitors to practise: 'You too can become a Rimpoche. All you have to do is start acting with wisdom and compassion.'

He was, above all else, unfailingly kind. When pressed about how to identify his incarnation, or *tulku*, Rimpoche said he must possess *maitrī*, friendliness. He had not, he said, developed any special *siddhis* or supernatural skills, whereby he could easily be identified, but he loved everybody. Only a boy with that quality would do.

As the contributions for this book have arrived, the spiritual stature of Dhardo Rimpoche has shone out from each piece. His perfection of the qualities of generosity, kindness, mindfulness, and selflessness are revealed again and again. These are qualities of a Bodhisattva, someone dedicated to the attainment of Enlightenment for the benefit of all sentient beings.

Rimpoche's qualities are timeless ones that are needed as much in our Western streets as in the hills of Kalimpong. They are not disembodied qualities, but need to take form to act as a light and an inspiration to those of us struggling with greed, hatred, and delusion in their manifold forms. In Dhardo Rimpoche these qualities took form; he was regarded by Sangharakshita, and by many of his students and followers in Kalimpong and elsewhere, as a living Bodhisattva and exemplar of Buddhist ideals.

This book aims to evoke these qualities of Dhardo Rimpoche, and to go beyond our concepts of space and time to bring the example of Dhardo Rimpoche to those who never met him, even to those who have never heard of him. The example of Rimpoche, and others like him, can live on in the imagination. We need not, in the words of Danavira, 'numb ourselves to them, thinking them dead and gone, after all, and make a barrier of our ignorance to their wisdom'.

A picture of Dhardo Rimpoche, necessarily incomplete, is built up piece by piece, by a number of contributors. Firstly, in chronological order of their meetings with him, there are offerings from members of the Western Buddhist Order who visited Rimpoche in Kalimpong, followed by three contributions from members of the Western Buddhist Order who met him not in the flesh but in their imagination. We then have a number of interviews conducted with those whose lives were enriched by living and working with Dhardo Rimpoche in Kalimpong, and who witnessed the daily effect of his practice. The book ends with a transcript of a talk given by Sangharakshita on the first anniversary of Rimpoche's death, 'The Message of Dhardo Rimpoche'.

Together these contributions add up to give us a picture of this Bodhisattva in human form – giving a sense of what it felt like to be the recipients of Rimpoche's attention, his love, and his care, and of how we might be inspired to bring those same qualities to life ourselves. Through these accounts we can 'meet' Dhardo Rimpoche, the greatly precious one of Dhartsendo, and let his gentle influence permeate our lives.

Through the publication of this commemorative book, may Dhardo Rimpoche's motto for the Indo-Tibet Buddhist Cultural Institute School spread more widely: 'Cherish the Doctrine, live united, radiate love.'

Sara Hagel
Birmingham
December 1999

from members of the Western Buddhist Order

Sangharakshita

Friendship implies a degree of mutual knowledge, and the fact that something like a friendship had begun to develop between Dhardo Rimpoche and me meant that we had got to know each other better. In Kalimpong this had hardly been possible, as we met only at intervals and usually on some formal occasion. Moreover, we were both rather reserved, whether by nature or as a result of having had, in his case, a Gelug monastic training, and in mine an English upbringing. None the less, each had definite feelings of good will towards the other, while from my side there was an appreciation of the Rimpoche's unusual qualities. That appreciation naturally increased during the tour, as well as in Delhi afterwards, when the fact that we were constantly together meant that I got to know him much better than before, even as he, no doubt, got to know me better. Though he had many positive qualities, the two that impressed me most were his uniform kindness and generosity and his unfailing mindfulness. The latter consisted not only in an entire absence of anything resembling forgetfulness or inattentiveness, but also in a degree of foresight and preparedness that was almost supernatural. In later years I was to say that Dhardo Rimpoche was never caught napping. On the tour itself there occurred an incident which strikingly exemplified this quality of his. The officials who were responsible for looking after the party and organizing its transport used to tell us each morning which places we would be visiting that day. One morning they told us we would be visiting a certain dam in the morning and in the afternoon, after returning to the train for lunch, a certain holy place. Unfortunately there was somehow a mix-up. An hour after leaving the train we found ourselves not at the dam, as we had expected, but at the holy place. This in itself did not really matter, but thinking that we would not be needing them until the afternoon none of us had brought any candles or incense sticks. None of us, that is, except Dhardo Rimpoche. As we were lamenting the fact that we would be unable to offer worship in the proper manner, he produced packets of candles and bundles of incense sticks from beneath his voluminous robes and smilingly distributed them among us. Strange to say, there proved to be enough candles and enough sticks of incense for everyone.[*]

[*] Sangharakshita, *In the Sign of the Golden Wheel,* Windhorse, Birmingham 1996

Lokamitra

In 1977 Surata and I arrived in Kalimpong after spending two weeks on pilgrimage in Sarnath, Bodh Gaya, Nalanda, and Rajagriha. My main reason for visiting Kalimpong was to make my *vandanā* (salutation) to the Venerable Dhardo Rimpoche. It was from him that Sangharakshita had taken the Bodhisattva vows, and since it is the spirit of the Bodhisattva Ideal that permeates and perfumes the whole of our Movement, as well as our individual practices, I felt a very strong link with Rimpoche even though I had never met him.

We presented Rimpoche with a *khata* (ceremonial scarf) on Sangharakshita's behalf, and then gave him our gifts – a selection of our publications for his library and an image of Vajrasattva made by Aloka. We gave him news of Sangharakshita and FWBO activities with the aid of a number of photographs. He was so happy to hear the news, and talked of Sangharakshita as his oldest friend in Kalimpong. But we were also charged with discovering his news for Sangharakshita – who had asked me to find out how the school was doing financially. It was quite clear that the school was now in difficulties as never before. To express his own appreciation, Sangharakshita himself had done some fund-raising for Rimpoche when he was in Kalimpong. Since the closing of the border with Tibet, Kalimpong – which had previously flourished on the trade between India and Tibet – had become a much poorer town. Support from the West had come almost to a standstill, partly because of inflation.

After leaving Rimpoche I really wanted to do something towards the continuation of his work, so on my return to the UK I decided to prepare an appeal on behalf of the school. (The school now continues to be funded by the Karuna Trust, a Buddhist-inspired charity supporting long-term social welfare work in aid of India's poorest communities.)

Sometimes we are lucky enough to come into contact with an individual who seems to be permeated by some higher dimension of consciousness, by the spirit of the Bodhisattva. In his presence our hard edges soften a little; we become more spiritually malleable, open, uplifted, and spiritually nourished. That is how I felt when I met Rimpoche. At the same time there was not the slightest trace of arrogance in him, no aura of mystery and confusion surrounded him. He was quite down-to-earth, practical, and straightforward, and so concerned for everyone and everything around him that one felt an immediate trust in him. Afterwards, on the plains, often with other Buddhists – monks and lay people – from whom I felt not the slightest trace of any higher dimension to their lives, I experienced, when recalling Rimpoche, that same feeling of spiritual refreshment.

Nagabodhi

Thanks to the vagaries of the Indian postal service I arrived at the ITBCI School unexpected. Rimpoche couldn't be found immediately, so a teacher took me on a tour of the school's classrooms, introducing me to successive batches of fascinated children. Time – mine and the teacher's – was short and conversation impossible, so within minutes I decided to do some filming. I was just delving into my bag when the door opened, and there was Rimpoche.

Arms outstretched he glided towards me, his face aglow with the warmest conceivable smile. It was the smile of a father, a mother, my best friend, and my dearest kindergarten playmate. In that smile, and in the oohs, aahs, and clucks that emanated from his mouth he seemed to respond with instant, precise love, not just to a visitor, but to me and my entire life so far.

There must have been 'formalities', but I can't remember them. Within moments he was clapping his hands and uttering gentle exclamations of wonder as I produced miniaturized gadgets (camera, cine-camera, and tape recorder) from my bag with a magician's flourish. As we played together he managed to explain (how?) that his translator could not be here for a while, and I suggested (how?) that he take me round the school, letting me film and photograph him among the children. This we did, and what struck me immediately was the happiness with which the kids greeted him as we passed from room to room. After all, this was the chief! Passing from one ramshackle building to another we discovered a tiny mite sobbing in an alleyway. Rimpoche left my side and gathered her in his arms, murmuring softly with real concern. Soon she was calm enough to answer his questions as he drew Tibetan characters on her little writing slate, coaxing her back to the human realm.

While I was filming an English class he was called away. A little later, nipping into his office for a fresh reel of film, I came across an extraordinary scene. Separated from an anxious mother and child by a desk strewn with teacups and frayed texts, Rimpoche intoned a chant as he focused absolute attention upon some dice-like objects in his hand. The boy was ill, I later discovered, and Rimpoche had been asked to provide a diagnosis.

We talked for ten hours. In conversation he was patient and precise, frequently checking that the most important points were surviving the two-way translation process. Whether talking about his life, the school, or a wide range of Dharma issues, he spoke in an even, forthright manner with complete if unobtrusive authority. When talking about Buddhist philosophy or practice his point of view was strictly and completely Tibetan. 'Rimpoche,' I asked after his tenth reference to hell, 'Does one really have to believe in hell to be a Buddhist?' My question clearly surprised him: 'But why else would one practise the Dharma?' he replied. While demonstrating complete fidelity to his native system, he was quite aware that it was a system appropriate to an already dying culture. We in the West, he said, would have to find our own way, develop our own systems. Had he been younger and in better health, he admitted, it was an adventure he would have loved to share.

Almost by accident I discovered that the school, which was in urgent need of repair and extension, had no financial backing, and was not even eligible for government grants. This was clearly worrying him considerably. There were so many ways in which he could have quite understandably hinted that the FWBO might like to help him, but beyond sharing his concerns with me as a friend he said nothing.

After four hours I ran out of recording tape. Delving into a cluttered drawer he produced another cassette. Clearly he was better prepared than I! When that tape came to an end he showed no inclination to terminate our interview, talking for another hour before inviting me back for dinner and more hours of talk later on.

Our encounter took place over a series of five sessions. Far from being disruptive, this gave me time to absorb the impact of each conversation, and to enjoy a kind of maturing friendship with Rimpoche rather than a single meeting. Each time we came together the room, the air, the entire world felt – actually felt – somehow sweeter, as if permeated by a subtle form of honey. I had never experienced anything like it, and I haven't since.

As I made a parting salutation I realized that tears were running down my cheeks. Uttering a stream of reassuring, almost motherly 'aahs', he bathed me for the last time in a palpable current of love. His eyes, I noticed, were moist too.

Kulananda

In 1982 I made my first visit to India. As well as trying, somewhat unsuccessfully, to do some buying for Windhorse Trading, I also visited TBMSG in Poona and then made a short pilgrimage: Sarnath, Bodh Gaya, and on to Kalimpong, to see Dhardo Rimpoche.

The journey from Bodh Gaya to Kalimpong by overcrowded second-class sleeper is arduous. You first travel south-east to Calcutta and then north to Siliguri, where you catch a bus up into the hills. It was few days' journey in all. In 1982, you had first to get a permit to stay in Darjeeling – the area was still 'sensitive' following border clashes with China in the 1950s. From Darjeeling you could apply for a permit to visit Kalimpong, but you could stay there for only one night.

It was cold in Darjeeling that March, and I was unprepared, having come up from the baking plains. The mountains were mostly hidden by a veil of mist and the town itself seemed to be living out the last dregs of its faded hill station glory. Still, there were Tibetans about, and gompas (monasteries), and it was not too unpleasant waiting for the authorities to issue a permit. I decided to buy a small rūpa of my yidam, Avalokiteśvara. If I was lucky, Rimpoche might bless it for me. But prices were higher than I had expected, my funds were low, and in the end, after much searching, I was able only to find a not particularly fine silver-alloy image with not much silver at that.

The next day my permit came through, and that afternoon I disembarked from the jeep in the bazaar in Kalimpong, slightly nauseated and bewildered after some reckless driving. A circus was in progress on the maidan, in what was without doubt the tattiest circus tent I have ever seen. On pilgrimage, everything one experiences is said to be symbolic. What did that circus, I wondered, say about my mental state?

After some searching, and with much help from friendly locals, I eventually located the ITBCI School and made my way to the office, where Jampel Kaldhen greeted me kindly. He went to fetch Rimpoche.

What now? I wondered. Would I be able to offer the khata without fluffing it? What would I say to him? Oh dear, why was I here, taking up his precious time?...

Before long, Rimpoche appeared. It is a shock to meet in the flesh someone you know so well from photographs. I was flustered, fluffed the offering, and was soon lost for words. Rimpoche quickly put me at my ease. 'I am so glad you have come,' he said, 'I'm sorry I never recognized you.'

Never recognized me? What did he mean?

'I have a few things to do now,' he went on, 'Please take a walk around Kalimpong for a while. Come back in a few hours' time. Then we can talk and you can ask me any questions you want.'

So I walked about the town. I looked at Dudjom Rimpoche's magnificent gompa with its splendid Padmasambhava murals, failed to find Sangharakshita's old vihara, and mused.

What should I ask Rimpoche? This man was a Lharampa geshe, one of the most learned Buddhists of his generation, and he had offered to answer any of my questions. What did I really need to know? And why was I here? After a week of uncomfortable travelling, what did I really want?

When I returned to the school, Rimpoche was sitting in the office with the smiling Ventrul Rimpoche, a former pupil of the school, now perhaps in his mid-twenties. Ventrul would translate. I groped for a meaningful question, and then gave up.

'Rimpoche,' I said, 'thank you so much for your time, and for your offer to answer my questions. I do appreciate it. But I have no questions. Sangharakshita has taught us all so well that there is nothing I feel I need to know. I have more than enough knowledge. All I need to do is practise. I just wanted to see you, really, and to thank you for all you have done. Especially for teaching Sangharakshita, who has passed things on so clearly to us.'

Rimpoche laughed with delight. 'Yes!' he agreed, 'I too am grateful. I am so glad I had the chance to meet and teach Sangharakshita. He has been able to teach in the West in a way that I myself never would have been able to.'

And so we passed a happy time, rejoicing in Sangharakshita's many merits.

'I miss him,' said Rimpoche. 'Since he left Kalimpong there has been nobody I could talk to as I talked with him....'

'Is there anything I can do for you, Rimpoche?' I asked, preparing to leave.

'No, since the Karuna Trust has started to help the school I need nothing,' Rimpoche replied. 'But perhaps you could try to help Ventrul Rimpoche instead.' That was typical of his thoughtful generosity.

Just before leaving, I brought out my rūpa of Avalokiteśvara. 'Can you please bless this for me, Rimpoche?'

'Hmm...' He looked at it, clearly not impressed with the craftsmanship. 'But it has no base. There is nowhere for the blessing to "take..."'

I must have looked crestfallen. 'Just give it to me,' he said, 'and come back tomorrow before you leave.'

The next morning I made my way back to the school. Rimpoche came down and handed me the rūpa. It had a small scarf about it, and was slightly heavier and quite warm. I looked at the base. Rimpoche had filled it up. Then he'd made a cardboard seal for it, covered that with some saffron-coloured cloth, glued it down, and sealed it with a cardboard cut-out double dorje.

I was ecstatic.

'Oh, Rimpoche! Thank you so much! What have you put in it?'

'Oh, mantras, incense, relics....'

'Mantras, incense, relics ... but ... what mantras? What....'

'Just mantras.' Rimpoche was not going to answer all my questions.

Such kindness. He must have stayed up very late to do that. For a total stranger, who arrived on his doorstep out of the blue, without even a question to ask. I felt deeply blessed. Even the jeep ride back to Darjeeling couldn't wipe the grin from my face.

But what did Rimpoche mean, when he apologized for not recognizing me? I don't know. And it doesn't matter.

Malini

In 1997 I spent a solitary retreat at Sudarshanaloka in New Zealand. The highlight of the retreat, perhaps also its very foundation, was my daily pilgrimage to the stupa containing some of Rimpoche's ashes. Climbing the hill that was painful to climb I saw this magnificent white form towering into the cold blue sky surrounded by puffy white clouds.

I immediately saw Rimpoche's eyes, then thought I was just seeing the eyes that appear on Nepalese stupas. Then I realized again, no, these eyes were slanted like Rimpoche's, they were his eyes. I felt the care and compassion pouring out of them, as I had felt from his human form. I felt streams of tears pouring down my cheeks, and remembered that when I visited him in 1982 one of my friends had been unable to stop herself from crying in his presence. As his English was limited, he had not been able to talk with her about it, but the kindness that exuded from him was enormous. He said, in what I felt to be a slightly perplexed way, 'Some people cry when they are happy.' My friend certainly was not a happy person then, and I figured even he could be wrong.

I realize now that he had probably been right. The tears that were rolling down my cheeks were not tears of sadness but tears of joy – like water flowing from an icicle on being exposed to the sun. The sun of Rimpoche's presence, his kindness, his compassion, his radiance and magnitude, thawed the coldness of my being and transported me into another realm. I found myself repeating his motto – 'Cherish the Doctrine, live united, radiate love' – and promising to try to practise this more diligently in my life, before circumambulating his stupa, chanting the Prajñāpāramitā mantra and reciting the *Ratnaguṇasaṁcayagāthā*.

I kept having memories of Rimpoche taking us to meet the children in their dormitories doing last-minute preparations for their exams. He told us they were a little anxious, but despite this their faces totally lit up on seeing him. It was clear they adored him and that they forgot their anxiety at least while he was there. I felt intense gratitude for having met Rimpoche in this life and that here he was, with us, at this stupa in New Zealand.

Vijayamala

When I met Rimpoche in 1983, I was struck by his free spirit, his spontaneity, his joy, and his kindness. When later I read about his rigorous training and daily routine I was a little taken aback. In the West, we do not normally associate freedom with such discipline. Yet, every day, Rimpoche followed a regular routine of about six hours' intensive meditation practice and ritual performances, from 4 a.m. until 10 a.m., with another few hours in the evening.

He saw these practices as an essential basis for the development of insight and compassion – the basis from which everything else in his life derived. Rimpoche stressed that he put many, many hours of practice, every day of his life, into becoming precious, becoming free. The practices allowed him to be free – free of the tyranny of a dissipated, undisciplined mind, of what we might call the ego. His commitment was to share that with others throughout his life. Certainly, by the time I met him, he seemed completely unpreoccupied. He was happy just to look at me and my companions for what seemed like an eternity. He was equally attentive to the young boy who was called to play to us – on a roughly-strung instrument that sounded like droplets falling off Himalayan icicles in spring-time – and to each of the children to whom he introduced us in our tour of the school. He was also happy to chat away, telling us now about his travels, now about some of his previous rebirths, and now about the neon revolving prayer-wheel on a shelf! But whether the topic was reminiscences or plastic mechanisms there was that quality of total concentration, the like of which I have not seen since.

This inner freedom, this egolessness, had its effect on his outward words and deeds. He lived free of real conflict with others, because he was free from the biases or worldly winds – the pulls and pushes of pleasure and pain, loss and gain, praise and blame, obscurity and fame – that motivate those of us caught up with the concerns of the ego. Rimpoche, beyond these biases of ego, had nothing to fear from the worldly winds, and so was able to come into real contact with his fellow human beings.

He took us into his personal quarters where every day he would meditate and study. Around the walls and in glass cabinets there were pictures and statues of various Buddhas and Bodhisattvas; wrathful figures with bulging eyes and halos of flames, alongside calm, seated figures with beautiful faces. There was also a painting of Rimpoche in one of his previous rebirths. He gave us each a little visiting-card with 'Dhardo Rimpoche Tulku' inscribed in curly lettering. For someone really quite new to the mysteries of Tibetan Buddhism the naturalness with which he shared these details of his daily practice was disarming. He wasn't showing off or making a point, just sharing with us things that were both very meaningful and an ordinary and integral part of his life. It was a perfect introduction to the Tantra.

Anyone who met Rimpoche would immediately be struck by his profound but unostentatious kindness. When I was preparing to meet him I did not know what to expect. I knew he was someone for whom my own teacher had the utmost respect. I found my own teacher hard enough to fathom; how was I to take this teacher of my teacher? In addition, I had never met an incarnate lama before. In the end I didn't need to 'take' him any way at all. He seemed so ordinary, yet extremely attentive and generous – with his time and his reminiscences as well as with the school's meagre facilities. Looking back, what I find extraordinary is that, with all my scrutiny, my desire to find a nice new category of 'incarnate lama' in which to place him, there was simply nothing for me to get hold of. Instead, I just had to sit there, somehow thrown back on myself by his ordinariness, my expectations rather painfully wriggling on dry land.

Rimpoche was taking us in. We were among the first of his Western visitors, and he was intrigued by the fact that we had flown half way across the world in less than a day inside a metal box. He saw us as travellers and compared our journey with the ordeal of his precarious trek across the Himalayas; a bit like comparing a trip on a luxury liner with single-handed sailing on the Southern Ocean. He gave us a string of dried cheese each, traditional gifts to travellers, though he warned us not to eat it as it was probably rancid! It was a strange feeling to be taken in so fully. Something like falling through space. At once frightening and exhilarating. I found myself struggling to hang on to the superficial elements of the conversation, but at the same time wanting to let go into this new territory; this tremendous spaciousness that was opening up as a result of such complete concentration.

It was Sangharakshita who first brought to our attention Rimpoche's message of 'Cherish the Doctrine, live united, radiate love.' Sangharakshita pointed out that radiation takes place from a central point that by definition has no magnitude. Rimpoche's love radiated out, and, as far as I am concerned, still radiates out, from a central point which has no magnitude at all. There are no impurities to get in the way; what is left is therefore an uninterrupted stream of compassion that radiates across time and through space. I think being exposed to this for those few days had the effect of subtly rearranging my constituent parts. I now have a constant reference point in my memory of Rimpoche. When I get too literal about things, or I find myself looking for that big spiritual experience, I can bring to mind the extraordinary ordinariness of his presence. This gives me an almost tangible sense of what it could feel like to be at the same time full of emotion and yet completely un-self-referential. I know it's possible, I've seen it.

Satyapala

I am very grateful for the chance to contribute to this celebration of the life and work of Dhardo Rimpoche. I was lucky enough to meet him on two occasions (in 1984 and 1986) and to correspond with him for a number of years and in the process develop a strong heart-link with him.

Our first meeting had very strong associations with death and ritual. I arrived in Kalimpong on the appointed day and went straight to his school only to find that he had been called away. A young woman in her thirties had died of tuberculosis and he was preparing for the death ceremony, so our meeting was delayed for half a day. I spent the night at Deki Lodge, well known by many FWBO travellers for its hospitality, and was awoken early the next morning by what at first seemed a very confusing and cacophonous sound. There were trumpets, lots of people speaking at once, and even some chanting. All this passed my hotel window as I lay there, still half sleep. It would have been easy to let the sound drift away and drop off to sleep again, but fortunately I realized that this was probably the procession for the death ceremony that Rimpoche would be conducting that morning. I dressed quickly and walked up Tirpai Hill in the direction of the sound. Towards the top of the hill the death ceremony was already in progress. What an experience. Up on a slight hillock stood Rimpoche, performing a puja with two other lamas. There was a big stupa on another small hill, and slightly lower down stood a chimney. I stood there rather shyly among the trees, watching the ceremony and this young woman being loaded into the top of the chimney. It seems that Tibetan women are cremated upright, while men are cremated sitting down.

The body once interred, a fire was lit in the chimney and the puja continued. After a while, a human chain was formed between the Rimpoches and the chimney and various offerings were blessed by the lamas and passed hand to hand down to the fire. At this point the relatives insisted that I join in, so I had the very moving opportunity to participate in the death ritual of this young Tibetan woman and to see Dhardo Rimpoche in a way that I could never have planned.

Later in the day came the first of several meetings with Rimpoche. I was there on behalf of the charity Aid For India (now the Karuna Trust) so a lot of our discussions, especially during that first visit, were connected with project planning for the school's new classrooms. But on my second visit I asked questions about Rimpoche's life, which were tape recorded and later used by Suvajra in his biography of Rimpoche.

In this short remembrance of Dhardo Rimpoche's life I would like to draw attention to just two or three of his many qualities. To begin with, when I interviewed Rimpoche in his apartment above the school, I was struck by his attentiveness and concentration. He had this wonderful habit: I would ask him a question – be it on the Dharma, the school, or his lifestyle – and he would look down and tightly scrunch up his eyes. For what sometimes seemed like a minute, he would sit there quietly, eyes scrunched up, the tape recorder running, and all of a sudden he would open his eyes and start talking to his secretary in Tibetan, who then translated.

His attentiveness was wonderful to behold, although it did go against me on one occasion. On my first visit I was rather surprised that every time he had a drink it seemed to be Nescafé, not, as I would have expected, Tibetan tea. I remember at a lighter moment pointing this out to him and saying that I had never drunk Tibetan tea. I do wish I'd kept my mouth shut because, before I could catch a breath, he got his secretary to rush off to his wife who immediately made me some Tibetan tea, consisting mainly of salt, yak's butter, plus, of course, tea – definitely an acquired taste!

In addition to his attentiveness and concentration, another quality that impressed me was the strength of his devotion and practice. Rimpoche lived his practice from the moment of his awakening to the moment he went to sleep. Whilst cleaning his teeth in the morning he would chant a mantra, when going to the toilet he would visualize a deity, indeed at all times of his waking day and, for all I know, while he was sleeping, he lived and breathed his practice.

Of all Rimpoche's qualities by far the most striking was his great natural generosity and kindness. I don't think it would be overstating the case to say that, rather than having to practise generosity and kindness like most of us, Rimpoche seemed to have become kindness itself. Generous activity seemed to be a natural expression of his very being. On my second visit this quality was brought home to me in a very personal and even shocking way.

We had already exchanged farewells. With a mixture of deep sadness, but also pleasure at having had the chance to visit him a second time, I said goodbye to Rimpoche, and to Jampel Kaldhen and his wife, and now some of the children escorted me back to Deki Lodge to pick up my belongings. Arriving at the Lodge I was shocked to find that Rimpoche had sent a boy ahead who was trying to pay my accommodation fees. Such an unnecessary act for a travelling Westerner who had what to a local would seem like unlimited riches of rupees! But in offering this needless act of generosity I felt that Rimpoche was holding up a mirror to me, that a poor lama was showing this brash, young, privileged Westerner a teaching in generosity that could not but pierce my heart. I felt positively humiliated. In his life Dhardo Rimpoche had been a great scholar, he had developed the Mahayana Temple at Bodh Gaya, he had built the ITBCI School, he was my teacher's teacher, but most of all, echoing the words of Ānanda at the time of the Buddha's death, Rimpoche was so kind. And as I left Kalimpong for the second and final time I knew then, if I hadn't realized it already, that I had been in the company of a very great man.

Ratnaketu

Kalimpong lay quiet as the Nepalese cook led me silently through the dusky streets to a small gate, down some crumbling stairs, and past a clump of bamboos to the few faintly-lit buildings that formed the ITBCI School. Once I had descended the stairs and gone inside, things started to happen rather quickly. In a blur of colour, smiles, and bows, two rather different worlds came into contact. Jampel, head of the school and Rimpoche's assistant, kept bowing and making unfamiliar gestures of welcome. In his smile and bright eyes, I glimpsed an awareness of the occasion too late to prepare me for what was to follow. Suddenly Rimpoche was there, standing right in front of me, slightly bowed, beaming friendly greetings, with his broad stubbled head inclined towards me and his hands together. It was a greeting more welcoming, happier, and more direct than I had ever experienced before – and it shocked me. I was an uncultured country boy suddenly in the presence of something unexpected, something much, much, more…. I was painfully aware that I didn't have the skill, the grace, the words, or the deeds to respond adequately to what I encountered.

Not knowing what to think, say, or do, I stood amazed by Rimpoche's welcome. Quickly Rimpoche and Jampel came to my rescue and I found myself seated on the edge of the couch at the end of the room. Rimpoche, too dazzling to look at, sat glowing with love and awareness at the other end of the couch. Obviously very happy, his legs tucked up beneath him, Rimpoche rocked slowly backwards and forwards, smiling, looking, and taking me in, his old hands resting softly in each other. How strange I felt; my hair didn't seem mine, my face didn't 'fit', nor my clothes….

Rimpoche just laughed, then he smiled, then we both laughed. Relaxing I unpacked the many gifts that friends had entrusted me with. One of the presents was a large photograph of the planet Earth, taken from space, distributed by the Hundredth Monkey Network – a peace group I had co-founded with friends in New Zealand. Looking at a photograph of the full sphere of the earth has a profound effect on many people and we were keen for Dhardo Rimpoche to have the opportunity to see it. Rimpoche was clearly moved. He spent a long time gazing at the picture, shaking his head and making quiet exclamations of wonder.

Rimpoche handled each gift in such a way as to magnify a hundredfold the *mettā* with which it was given. The utmost delicacy and care with which he examined everything amazed me. It was as if even the sturdiest of objects were fragile, and the simplest of gifts contained hidden truths – so intently did he admire them. Jampel, who likewise handled everything with gratitude and tender care, placed all the little offerings upon the shrine that stood against the side wall. They were still there when I visited again ten years later. I remembered the impression my friend Purna had gained on his visit to Kalimpong a few years earlier; that Rimpoche was the kindest person he had ever met.

I asked Rimpoche some pressing questions. He told me that after Enlightenment, friendships are continued on the *samboghakāya* level; that I should develop my sādhana from small beginnings, then slowly expand it; he warned me of the obstacles that can arise if one goes off on one's own, and pointed out that in the cities there is a great need for the Dharma. I told Rimpoche about a statue of Tārā I had seen in Darjeeling, which seemed to be made of iron and looked like Khadiravani, the Green Tārā, except that, from a skull-cup or bowl in her left hand, resting in her lap, arose a flame. Rimpoche shocked me with his response. It was clear that for him, even hearing a description of a Bodhisattva is a coming into their presence. He involuntarily displayed subtle gestures of respect, and told me, in tones that communicated decades of devotion, that she was a wrathful Tārā. 'Wherever there are flames, there is wrath,' Jampel translated. Without speaking, Rimpoche showed me that the wrathful deities are to be treated with a degree of respect that I can hardly imagine.

Upon learning that my sādhana is Prajñāpāramitā, Rimpoche told me he was glad that sādhanas like that are being practised in the West. When I asked him if he would bless the image of Prajñāpāramitā I had recently purchased in Darjeeling, he was happy to oblige. It was getting late as Jampel showed me out and instructed me to return in the morning to collect the rūpa and say farewell.

The next day I was to be even more amazed. Again Jampel ushered me with unfamiliar respect into the reception room and the presence of Dhardo Rimpoche, who greeted me with warmth, friendliness, joy, and respect. Rimpoche returned my rūpa, now empowered, and showed me how to wrap her up in a piece of gold cloth, with cotton wool to protect her face. I felt wrapped in Rimpoche's mettā as he showed me those simple things. To my surprise, Rimpoche unfurled, and then presented to me, a small thangka. 'A good artist,' Jampel translated. It was Prajñāpāramitā; her yellow, four-armed form. She had a blue and gold aura and the green nimbus of a fully enlightened one, appearing on a pink lotus, in a landscape of tall green mountains and blue lakes. Her first pair of hands held a golden vajra and a Dharma text raised to shoulder height. Her other hands held a vase of initiation in her lap, said to contain the blessings of all the Buddhas. Her three eyes stared penetratingly at the viewer.

As amazing as Rimpoche's generosity was, it was not yet exhausted. Somehow, Rimpoche found time to compose and type a letter addressed to the Auckland Chapter of the Western Buddhist Order. Rimpoche told Jampel, who told me, that in the letter Dhardo Rimpoche expressed thanks for the many gifts we had given him, saying that the large photograph of the Earth reminded him of śūnyatā (emptiness), and he presented us with a gift of a vajra and a bell, symbols of wisdom and compassion. Once again, Rimpoche's kindness and generosity astounded me.

After the taking of photographs, and having said a reluctant farewell, I received Dhardo Rimpoche's blessing – in the form of a khata placed around my neck. As I left,

Jampel told me that Rimpoche had meditated and chanted long into the night, blessing the little figure of Prajñāpāramitā. Dazed, I stumbled out on to the path to stand for a while just looking back at the building in which Dhardo Rimpoche, the Bodhisattva from Dhartsendo, dwelt. It seemed to me that the whole school was permeated by love, love and awareness of which Dhardo Rimpoche is but the biggest and purest channel and which finds a thousand openings in response to him.

Suvajra

My first visit to Dhardo Rimpoche took place in the context of a pilgrimage or, rather, it was the culmination of a pilgrimage. The 'external' pilgrimage was, I knew, coming to a climax: Sarnath, Bodh Gaya, Nalanda, and now Dhardo Rimpoche. However, a true pilgrimage is never external, it is an inner experience and exploration, and no amount of planning or organization dictates the experiences that come your way, nor is there any guarantee what you will make of them afterwards. The 'meaning' of my own pilgrimage was still unclear, although I could feel a force deep inside me rising ever nearer the surface, bringing with it previously buried motivations.

Sangharakshita had never been happy for members of his order to take initiation from Tibetan lamas. (This is not the place to go into all the reasons; suffice it to say that Tibetan lamas work firmly within the 'Tantric' tradition and, unlike Sangharakshita, see their practices as the pinnacle of the Buddhist system.) But he was happy for some Order members to undergo initiation into a meditation practice specifically from Dhardo Rimpoche. He thought of the connection thus made with Dhardo Rimpoche as being a further inspiration to practise, rather than being given a 'higher' meditation practice. All this he told me – but only after I had returned from my meeting with Dhardo Rimpoche!

I wanted Dhardo Rimpoche to give me initiation into a meditation practice, yet I found my emotions in turmoil due to self-doubt. I doubted my motivation and I doubted views. Was it that I wanted initiation as a 'thing' to take away in my pocket and to play with afterwards or, worse, display to others? Did it really come down to this?

Was there nothing in my motivation more positive than this? All the questions about initiation I had ever asked Sangharakshita flashed before me.

Sangharakshita's opinion had been that it is far better to have one main visualization practice and stick with that for several years, if not for life. I put this to Dhardo Rimpoche and he agreed that this was by far the best approach, rather than have commitments to visualize so many Buddhas and Bodhisattvas that one made little progress with any of them. Yet I still wanted to ask Dhardo Rimpoche for initiation.

Sangharakshita, I recollected, had also said that initiation was not a 'thing' at all. It was just a special form of communication, and that if communication was to be real communication it should, most likely, contain an element of initiation! There was really no 'initiation' as such, just a communication from a person who had some experience of a certain thing to someone who did not have that experience, which acted as a sort of spark or inspiration. Having sorted out in my mind this fundamental point, I asked myself whether I was up to that sort of communication? I wasn't so sure.

Rimpoche was still looking at me. Perhaps a minute of silence had already passed in which all eyes had been on me – Rimpoche's, Jampel's, and Mrs Kaldhen's. In my mind's eye huge chunks of my life floated past me. It was as if I was not only reviewing parts of myself but also in those few moments trying to do a 'spring clean'. I was trying to effect a change in motivation. Was it even possible in these few moments to change my motivation, I wondered? Finally, I thought that if I did genuinely recognize these motivations for what they actually were, the process of change was already on its way and I could in fact leave it up to Rimpoche to decide.

However, Mrs Kaldhen stepped forward and anxiously said something – no doubt about the meal, which was probably going cold somewhere. At that moment I decided to back out of my decision. No, the time was not right! Jampel started to say something too, but Rimpoche, seeing something was going on in me and that I was not yet finished, motioned them both to wait. Rimpoche's eyes were so encouraging. I took the opportunity. I said to Rimpoche that, even though I felt I wasn't ready, human life being so precarious, it may not be my good fortune to ever meet him again, and that since he was well qualified and I felt great devotion to him would he consider communicating a meditation practice to me?

Rimpoche gasped, doubled over, put his head in both hands and groaned. 'Oh no!' I thought, 'What have I done? I have said the wrong thing! Oh no! Oh no!' I was in mental agony – all the insecure, unconfident, parts of me erupted. Indeed, what had I done? There was Rimpoche still bent over after half a minute, still making various noises, which in my state of mind I could only interpret in the worst possible way. 'Nobody had told me to expect this! He could have just said no! What had I done?' Finally he sat up and asked Kaldhen to fetch a small, silver, lidded container. He removed one end, took out some dice, and proceeded to throw them into the maroon velvet of the lid. He did this several times over and then asked, via Jampel, which meditation practices I already did. He then continued to shake the dice but this time, like some gambler shaking for a treble six, he put his cupped hands to his mouth and blew on them. It seemed no luck! He tried repeatedly, blowing on them, pressing them to his temples and, as I thought, willing a treble six. Still no luck. He did this about twenty-five times in all. In the end he fetched a text across, looked up some tables, and asked how old I was. Getting the right line with his finger he looked up and, smiling, said in English 'Green Tārā!' Now it was my turn to gasp. I thought he had still been trying to decide if it was appropriate, but really he had been trying to decide which practice. I asked in Tibetan, 'Dolma?' unable to believe my ears. This time he said 'Green Dolma!' The secretary confirmed, 'Yes, Green Tārā!' Rimpoche said that now the most important thing was the giving of this practice, and that we would do that first thing next morning.

Mrs Kaldhen now seized her chance. I interpreted the Tibetan 'Please, please, it is time to eat!' – it sounds the same in all languages when said by an anxious mother!

Moksananda

'You must attain the bodhicitta, you need to have compassion.' Dhardo Rimpoche had his eyes screwed up and his thick short eyebrows almost merged where he frowned. His long wispish moustache and the few scruffy hairs beneath his lower lip mesmerizingly focused my attention on his words, at the same time inadvertently causing a certain revulsion. Shaven-headed, wrapped in maroon and yellow robes, he looked down at his translator, his eyebrows suddenly raised and parted, his eyes a little watery. Then he turned to the rest of us, looking to see if we'd understood.

My first impression of Rimpoche, as he emerged in his monk's robes, walking down the stone steps that led into the school courtyard, was of an old man, older and more stooped than I had imagined, and, at least in that moment, tired. He briefly greeted Suvajra, one of my companions, with the raise of a hand, before climbing the steps that ran up the side of the stone building along the courtyard. Somewhat hesitant, we followed him up, then waited before entering, allowing him to settle himself into his room.

All yellows and reds, thangkas and cloths and rugs, butter lamps and incense, the room glowed in the clear Himalayan light. At the far end, between a shrine with silk flowers and a window with a fine ironwork grating, sat a squat and cushioned sofa-like chair draped with blankets. Before it stood a low table, covered with cloth, and before that stood Dhardo Rimpoche, wrapped in maroon, a short man by Western standards and physically frail. He calmly accepted our prostrations, khatas, and words of greeting, and directed us to take a seat. He himself sat upon the sofa-like chair, behind the low cloth-covered table upon which lay papers, bowls, and perhaps a bell.

Suvajra told him we were hoping to video an initiation and he seemed well disposed to the idea. I asked him if there existed a Five Buddha Mandala practice, but he thought not. He could perhaps compose one himself, of course, but that would take much preparation, time, and effort. Finally it was decided that he would initiate Moksapriya into the Vajrasattva practice. My friend seemed rightly pleased.

It was agreed that we would do the ritual the following morning and it was then, as the afternoon drew on, that we sat before him while he urged us to develop bodhicitta (the compassionate desire to attain Enlightenment for the sake of all sentient beings). 'If the bodhicitta has arisen, everything will be all right; there is no need to worry about anything.' He sat looking down at us all – with that friendly, unwavering look.

'How might we do that, Rimpoche?' He nodded slowly, as if pleased with the question, then screwed up his eyes once more and spoke in Hindi. 'Recognize all beings as your mother, realize how kind she has been....' Rimpoche led us through the six traditional stages of developing the bodhicitta and I thought of my mother. 'A lotus flower is born in muddy water but is not polluted by it. We are born in saṁsāra, but we need not be of it.' Had we understood?

Back at the hotel we talked little, slept early, and dreamt. I fell into a bottomless abyss, fell and fell, down and down, and suddenly made a fantastic discovery, of a certain state of mind in which I could stop my falling and even float upwards on a current of hot air rising within the abyss. So high up could I float that finally I was able to take hold of the clouds and pull myself completely clear! The landscape was rocky and rough and I found myself with others, many people, friends I had picked up on the way. To my delight they all played on musical instruments. Playing and dancing, this band of friends accompanied me to a nearby castle, high up on the rocks, from where I had departed many years before. There I saw others whom I knew, and recognized many as children now grown up. Yet they didn't seem to recognize me. And a woman from the castle was looking for a precious stone, a stone which only I knew how to find, so we set off on an expedition headed by my band of friends, who joyfully played their special brand of Tibetan reggae.

That next morning it turned out that Rimpoche intended to initiate all four of us into the Vajrasattva practice. I had been given the Vajrasattva practice by Sangharakshita at the time of my ordination, and certainly felt no need to be 'initiated' again. But I could see no harm in accepting Rimpoche's offer and took it to be a blessing that would not only strengthen my connection with Vajrasattva but with Rimpoche too. Vajrasattva, as understood within the Western Buddhist Order, is known as the Adibuddha, the primordial Buddha who represents primordial purity, and is of course pure white in colour.

Things were not to be quite as we had expected, however. Arriving at the school we were joined, much to our surprise and delight, by a Tibetan lama who, on hearing about the initiation that Rimpoche was to bestow, had asked to receive it too. Jampel told us to wait while Rimpoche finished his preparations. He had, apparently, begun the previous night, soon after we had left him for our hotel, and since the very early morning had been preparing the ritual offerings and butter lamps as well as undertaking whatever practices and pujas were necessary. I felt slightly ashamed that we were putting him, and Jampel too, to so much trouble.

After a short wait, five of us made our way up the stone steps to Rimpoche's room, three Western Order members and one Indian, all dressed in the fluttering blue shirts of Indian Order members, and our Tibetan lama friend in his maroon robes. Sitting on the floor in a semicircle around the sofa-like chair upon which Rimpoche sat, and with the video camera rolling in the background, we listened attentively to his explanations. We began, on Suvajra's request, by chanting the Refuges and Precepts in Pāli and English, but then everything turned Tibetan and unknown and we falteringly chanted after Rimpoche while he carefully explained, through Aniruddha or Jampel, the significance of each stage. Rice was showered upon us, lamps were offered, a metal incense burner was passed around, smoking thickly, while each of us wafted and breathed in its unknown contents. And all the time Rimpoche chanted, striking *mudrās* (ritual gestures) in fluid rhythm, punctuating the proceedings with the sharp ring of the vajra-bell. We recited the Vajrasattva mantra three times, all the while thinking of Rimpoche as Vajrasattva, and the mantra poured from his heart into each of ours, where it stayed and dwelt so that even now we hold it for ourselves. As Rimpoche described Vajrasattva, 'Dorje Sempa', we learned that in this particular form he is not white, and the *hūṁ* at his heart not blue, but that both were yellow, a rich golden yellow.

What was left of the morning and the early afternoon was spent interviewing Rimpoche again, and in the late afternoon light, itself turning orange and yellow, we went through the practice that Rimpoche had given us. Telling us that the visualization and mantra recitation of Vajrasattva was particularly good for reaffirming our *samaya* (bond), he carefully taught us what acts made that *samaya* defective. Realizing by then that mine must be all but defunct, I was even gladder of my connection with the Diamond Being, and we saw that Vajrasattva, whilst embodying purity, also promoted increase, development, and even longevity, that the vajra-bell he held at his waist was *śūnyatā*, that the vajra he held to his heart was bodhicitta.

We had one more morning's interview and then, all too soon, we were forced to say our goodbyes to Dhardo Rimpoche. He presented us each with a khata, longer and more beautiful than any we had presented to him, and with a small signed photograph of himself, in which he appears dressed in gold-embossed yellow and orange Tantric robes, a long dark wig beneath a Bodhisattva's crown, sitting upon his sofa-like chair, displaying the *mudrā* of Vajrasattva. Bowing before him as he gave me khata and photograph, I could only find words from my heart and told him that I would always think of him with gratitude, respect, and love. He replied, simply and kindly, that he hoped the work at my Buddhist centre would prosper, and that he too would put me in his meditations.

I had entered a strange – even 'weird' – world to meet Dhardo Rimpoche, but I had no doubt that I had been given something that was not just of that world. I had been given something that, in essence at least, I could take back into my own world – indeed into any world. The man I had met was, according even to my own teacher, a living Bodhisattva, someone within whom the bodhicitta had arisen, and I had no reason to doubt that this was true. Indeed, this man had, in different ways, done nothing but exhort us to cherish, to develop, to attain, that bodhi heart.

Yet over the twelve years since our meeting there has been something that has always intrigued me, even puzzled me, a question that has always hovered around that figure of Dhardo Rimpoche. My teacher's own teacher, a highly respected tulku, a top Lharampa geshe who had gone on to attend one of the Tantric colleges in Lhasa, the abbot of Yi Ga Choling monastery, a living Bodhisattva in whom the bodhicitta had arisen, and, for me at least, the embodiment of Vajrasattva, Rimpoche had nonetheless dedicated the last considerable chunk of his life to the development of a small school for Tibetan refugees in a backwater of an Indian hill station known as Kalimpong. He did not, as far as I knew, have numerous disciples, or go on great teaching tours, but chose instead to work and live in a small community, helping children and friends who might or might not decide to take up spiritual practice. Either he was not what I thought he was, or my idea of the nature of a Bodhisattva, even of Vajrasattva, needed reassessing. Had I understood?

Well, of course, I hadn't, and, truth be known, I haven't. Yet largely through the example of Dhardo Rimpoche I have, I think, begun to sense that above all else a Bodhisattva works always in relation to others, that is, works in relation not to an abstract idea about others but to real people, with whom he or she is in real contact. A Bodhisattva, I suspect, experiences himself or herself as those relationships, relationships that spread out to include all beings everywhere, perhaps, but which are experienced and lived out with specific people in a specific time and place. Dhardo Rimpoche's loyalty to his school and to his people, to those with whom he was in daily contact, is what, above all else, has stayed with me all these years. I do not find it in the least surprising that it was in the midst of that loyalty and work, in the midst of his people, in the midst of his children, that my own teacher met him and enriched his own understanding of the Dharma – an understanding that now unfolds in the West. I do not find it strange that that meeting was to have such far-reaching consequences. Within the delightful, and perhaps mysterious, combination of Rimpoche as the embodiment of Vajrasattva, exhorting me to develop compassion, to give rise to the bodhicitta, and Rimpoche as a children's schoolmaster, there is, I suspect, a profound yet simple teaching for us all. And it is from within that enigmatic teaching that Rimpoche looks down even now, his long wispish moustache above a scruffy beard, his eyebrows raised, his eyes friendly and unwavering, if a little watery, and silently asks us if we have understood.

Manjusvara

Dhardo Rimpoche was even smaller than I had expected, perhaps no more than five feet tall. Although seventy-three and occasionally troubled with ill health, he conveyed a sense of deep strength. His mind seemed agile and fresh. Before he spoke he would screw up his eyes in concentration as if lost for words, although, really, he was reflecting carefully upon my questions. More than anything his answers displayed the deepest concern and compassion for the world about him. Being with him, I realized, was like being gently wrapped in a warm cloak of kindness.

I was meeting Dhardo Rimpoche in my capacity as editor of the *Karuna Trust Newsletter*, in order to report on the progress of the ITBCI School. The 200 pupils come from Kalimpong itself and further afield. Most are Tibetans, but some are Sherpas who speak the Tibetan language. Because Kalimpong is close to Tibet, the school is able to help the refugees who still occasionally cross the border into India. Ex-pupils have gone on to work in places as far away as Japan and Switzerland.

What, I wondered, could Tibetan culture teach the world at large? 'I particularly feel it can teach non-violence and compassion', Rimpoche explained, 'it is very important that we teach these things to children. If, for example, you see small children playing with insects, tearing their wings or hitting them with sticks, you must explain that this hurts the insects. They should learn that they don't have to hurt insects in order to enjoy themselves in the playground.' Rimpoche then searched through some papers and to my surprise produced a recent copy of *Time* magazine. He turned to an article surveying the attitudes of High School students in America. 'It makes me very sad to read that so many young people in the West are turning to drugs as a means of escape. They must feel a great emptiness in their hearts that they should try to fill them this way.' He continued: 'People feel that life is short. Because of this, instead of working for others, they just try to acquire wealth for themselves. But if we live in this way, we become isolated. Our lives become like bubbles on the surface of the water. But people can be inspired by action. If they see that something is happening they start to give.'

Rimpoche explained how he had started the school with virtually nothing. Things had built up very gradually indeed. People would give a few rupees, allowing him to buy paper and pencils. Then when they saw he was doing something useful with their money they offered more, so in this way they gradually helped the school to grow: 'If you work hard in the right way it will spread like light.'

The light of Rimpoche's work had obviously spread very effectively indeed. Our fund-raising appeals back in Britain had brought in enough money to pay for the erection of two major buildings housing classrooms, boarding facilities, and staff quarters, as well as providing funds to pay the staff more realistic salaries. The long-term future of the school was finally secure.

After all his years of experience with children, would he have any advice to give to parents of children in the West? 'Yes. They should teach their children that actions have consequences. And they should teach them to respect their elders. In particular we should always remember our first teacher, the person who taught us our ABC and 1-2-3, for this person gave us entry into all the richness and beauty of human culture.'

A few hours after the interview, in the balmy night air, I stood in the courtyard with Jampel Kaldhen. We were looking at the almost completed block of classrooms and dormitories that Karuna's support was making possible. Suddenly the shadowy image of Dhardo Rimpoche appeared, stepping carefully between the builders' materials. As he peered at each new detail of the day's work he made faint murmuring sounds of approval. According to Jampel, Rimpoche made this little inspection each evening after dinner. My heart filled with delight to think that we had been able to help this wonderful man, who had devoted his life to the welfare of others.

Gunabhadri

A heart response to a photograph made me decide to visit Dhardo Rimpoche in 1989, three months before he died. It was in the context of a pilgrimage to the Buddhist sites in India that Sanghadevi and I spent nearly two days with Dhardo Rimpoche in Kalimpong.

Dhardo Rimpoche was a very small man physically. It was only when our meeting drew to a close and Dhardo Rimpoche turned around that I noticed how stooped his back was and how old and frail he looked. My experience of him had not been like that at all. He had seemed young and his spirit was one of unfailing kindliness. His actions, his every gesture, exuded mindfulness, pervaded by a strong sense of mettā and compassion. He seemed to radiate light. Golden light. He was light. That is what I saw.

I asked him to bless a small image of Tārā and he agreed to do this in the context of a Tsongkhapa puja he would be performing that very night. (Though he gave us much of his time, it was obvious he was very busy, keeping long hours late into the night.) When I handed him my Tārā rūpa he examined her, paying attention to every detail and looking at her with an expression of kindliness, full of mettā. The strange thing is that, while he was so occupied, I started to feel like Tārā. That is the only way I can describe it. I felt completely seen and accepted on a very deep level. I was very happy.

Sanghadevi and I asked many questions. We asked, Jampel translated, Dhardo Rimpoche answered, and Jampel translated. When I asked about Tārā, a lot of information passed back and forth at great speed between us. A very intense discussion took place on what mattered most to me. Dhardo Rimpoche explained an extended version of the Tārā practice, and whilst he was explaining it was as though he was in the presence of what he was describing, as though he saw in front of him the Buddha and Bodhisattva figures he was talking about. The effect upon me of Rimpoche's reply was to turn around my whole way of seeing. It was a recognition: 'Oh, is it like that!' I felt incredibly affirmed as though I was worthy of being given to. This connects with a very strong impression I had of Rimpoche: that he treated everything, from the highest to the lowest, as if it was divine. Everything was worthy of his attention, his mettā, his generosity. Although in spiritual stature he was very big, he was so humble, so ordinary, but to such a degree that it exuded a perfume of Buddhahood.

Apart from in a dream, in which Dhardo Rimpoche looked at me with his third eye open, I never saw Rimpoche again. Three months later – I was back in England on a solitary retreat – I was walking round a field reciting mantras when I began to hear and feel that I was in the presence of many Tibetan monks doing the same thing. That evening I received a message from a friend to tell me that Dhardo Rimpoche had died. Did I see snowdrops falling or was it blossom from the trees? That is what usually happens – according to Tibetan tradition – when a great monk dies. When I reflected that I would not meet Rimpoche any more, I looked at the Tārā image on my shrine, vibrating with light and his presence, and realized that I could always stay in touch with Rimpoche by practising and passing on what he had taught.

Sanghadevi

One of the first things that struck me about Dhardo Rimpoche was that he didn't put much weight on ceremony. Gunabhadri and I had decided beforehand that when we met him we would do full length prostrations – which we did, and which felt completely appropriate from our side – but I had a strong sense that for Rimpoche it was neither here or there, indeed he made a gesture indicating that it was not necessary. He was just very welcoming, and quickly made us feel at home.

Rimpoche had a very unassuming manner, yet there was a feeling of supreme confidence. Overall, though, I was struck by his kindness and generosity. He expressed this practically in the way he gave us his undivided attention for hours at a time. He was always intensely concentrated in conversation, especially when describing sādhanas. Whilst he was explaining aspects of the Green Tārā sādhana to Gunabhadri, I had the opportunity to observe him, and there were moments when, whilst Gunabhadri was listening to Jampel translating, Rimpoche would sit back for a few moments and sometimes look up, straight into my eyes, and we would exchange a look. I experienced this look as a powerful, penetrating knowingness, tinged with humour – there was often a sort of glint in his eyes. But there seemed to be a sense of frustration there as well, as if there was so much Rimpoche wanted to share and so little time in which to do it. He did express something to the effect that it was a shame we had so little time to spend with him. I formed the impression that he would do all he could to stay alive as long as he could, whilst there were people who wanted to visit him for teachings.

There were also lighter times, such as when we showed Rimpoche photographs, gave him gifts, or sat silently eating our meals. The gifts, from us and from others, really delighted him; he had an innocent childlike quality when opening them. His eyebrows would rise and he'd ooh and aah over them. He was particularly struck by a really fluorescent yellow mala (a Buddhist rosary used for counting mantras). He seemed quite taken and intrigued by this, perhaps because of the material (it was probably plastic) which looked quite unusual. Rimpoche said it would be useful for a certain Tantric ritual which needed malas of different colours, and it seemed he didn't have a yellow mala.

One of the things I brought to Rimpoche for him to bless was an initiation vase. It was a cheap, plain, initiation vase that I had bought in Darjeeling. As soon as I told Rimpoche that it was to be used for women's ordinations in the West, all his attention homed in on this vase. He rang his bell to summon Jampel, who went to fetch kusa grass and peacock feathers. Rimpoche spent some time carefully taking each piece of grass, measuring it to make sure all the pieces were the same length, and placing it in the vase. It was a quite a lesson for me. There I was with important questions to ask and aware that precious time was passing; and there he was putting this grass into this vase! Gradually my mental agitation calmed down, the grasping mind calmed down. I saw what he was doing and in that seeing I got a glimpse of what they call the 'vajra world'. Rimpoche had seen the significance of this vase and was treating this cheap, plain vase as precious – and it was becoming precious before my very eyes as so much love and attention went into it.

When it came to the final meal, I found myself feeling very sad and couldn't stop crying. Jampel was not around to translate and we were eating in silence. I had the strong sense that I had been given something very precious. I had been given so much kindness, care, and attention, and felt very much at home. The thought that I might not see Rimpoche again made me very sad. I saw Rimpoche as a precious gem (I didn't know at the time that Rimpoche meant 'precious one') and that in this world beings like him are very rare. Here I was with this little old man, in this very obscure place, but I had a sense that when he was no longer there it would be a loss to the whole of humanity, to the whole world. When Jampel came in I told him this and Rimpoche said that he too felt subdued.

Suddenly Rimpoche sprang up, went into his back room, and came back with the things he'd blessed for us, gifts for us and for others, and letters to take back. Suddenly it was just like Christmas (it was in fact almost Christmas) and the whole atmosphere lightened. Before long we were saying goodbye. Rimpoche looked at me and said in English, 'See you again.' I looked at him and said 'I hope so.' Again, he looked at me very directly and said 'Oh yes, yes.' When he said this I felt a tremendous peace, and I thought 'Yes, there is a connection. Yes, I might see you again.' I did think I might see him in this lifetime, but when he died I still felt those words were true. I've met Rimpoche and he still lives on in my mind and heart, as continued inspiration and encouragement. Through meeting him I felt a tangible deepening of faith, and a greater determination to embrace the path of the Bodhisattva. I feel tremendous gratitude for all Rimpoche has given me and continues to give to me through his life and his example.

Chittadhara

After a long and memorable journey, I was at last in Deki Lodge in Kalimpong. The school was not too difficult to find, and soon Jampel came down to receive me and took me to his office. 'You want to see Rimpoche?' 'Yes, I came to arrange a time....' 'Wait!' he said and dashed out of the room. He came back after a few seconds and asked if I wanted tea. The tea arrived before Jampel returned again and I had plenty of time to finish it. Then Jampel came back and I felt excited that at least we could fix a time. But no! Jampel said, 'Please come, Rimpoche can see you now.'

I did not expect this, and suddenly the bottom of my stomach seemed to disappear into the void. Panic! Stop! This is going too fast! 'How do I give the khata?' I quickly asked. 'Give it just like this.' Slowly but surely I was being led into the presence of Rimpoche, and I felt a curious mixture of anxiety and sudden happiness. I stepped into Rimpoche's reception room, walked up to him rather stiffly, and handed the khata to him with a bow, again rather stiffly. But there was nothing stiff about the delicate hands and arms that received the khata, nor about the most kind and amicable face that smiled at me. I was not filled with holy ecstasy, the light did not descend upon me from the sky (or perhaps it did but I just didn't see it), the earth didn't shake, but suddenly I felt quite happy and at ease.

At some point Jampel left the room to attend to some immediate business, and for a while I shared the room with Rimpoche alone. I do not speak Tibetan and Rimpoche did not speak English, so our communication for the moment became purely non-verbal – and what a communication we had. First of all we were just beaming good will and positive feeling towards each other, and then we made use of simple gestures. I resorted to the use of a few English words. Rimpoche made a joke (still non-verbally) and we both laughed at it. What made the situation so funny was Rimpoche's extremely expressive face and gestures. When he laughed his whole body gently shook, his shoulders rounded up as he looked at me, and opened his mouth to let out an indescribable laughter.

Whilst waiting for Jampel's translations, I had time to listen to Rimpoche speaking. His voice was very soft to the point of being almost inaudible. On the other hand he listened all the time very intently. He would not miss a word, even though he could not understand much of what I said. It was almost as if he was taking in every second, every moment, being completely receptive to what was going on. His replies were very thoughtful and precise and he would always think carefully before answering.

I left Kalimpong and I left India, but such a strong impression of Rimpoche remained in my mind that it seemed as though he did not leave me. Thousands of miles lay between us but I did not feel the weight of that separation. It seemed as though there was contact all the time. I thought of Rimpoche every day, and when I thought of him it seemed as though he was there with me, almost like a guardian angel, sometimes appearing in meditation, and sometimes simply being a beneficial influence.

Writing this down has been a strong experience for me, and my feelings have built up through such an intense reflection on Rimpoche that I am crying. I find it hard to understand how Rimpoche has had such strong influence on me, but this is undoubtedly the case.

Vessantara

I asked the boy beneath the pines.
He said, 'The master's gone alone
Herb-picking somewhere on the mount
Cloud-hidden, whereabouts unknown.'[*]

If one day I am taken seriously ill, in the ambulance I shall probably reach into my trouser pocket for something which is a kind of talisman for me – a symbol of my spiritual life. It is a mala that goes with me everywhere. I possess several malas. Some have beautiful beads and colourful tassels, or are made of scented wood. But the one that lives in my pocket has beads of cheap orange plastic, and a crude tassel of thick red cord. This is my constant companion, rather than its more beautiful rivals for my affection, because it was given to me by Dhardo Rimpoche.

I began corresponding with Rimpoche in the late eighties, at Sangharakshita's suggestion. The reply I received to my introductory letter was very warm and welcoming. Rimpoche particularly picked up on something that I had mentioned in my letter: that I was meditating on White Tārā (the female Bodhisattva who embodies the quintessence of compassion) for the benefit of Sangharakshita's long life. Rimpoche very strongly encouraged me in this. We agreed that I should come to Kalimpong so that he could instruct me in a new meditation practice that I wanted to take up. Unfortunately my father became ill with cancer, and it was two years before his condition seemed stable enough for me to go to India. Finally, in 1990, I travelled out with the late Arthadarshin (a very easy companion), and after a few weeks we found ourselves in Darjeeling, contemplating the ethereal bulk of Kanchenjunga.

[*] *Searching for the Hermit in Vain*, by Chia Tao (*777–841*), trans. Lin Yutang

In a state of nervous anticipation I travelled on alone to Kalimpong, and made my way to the ITBCI School. I was met by one of Jampel Kaldhen's family who told me at once that Rimpoche had been taken ill, and that he had been diagnosed as having had a stroke. In a state of numb disappointment I was taken into Rimpoche's empty room where I sat surrounded by his thangkas, and was given tea. Then the family invited me to meet Rimpoche.

It was a strange meeting, and not at all the joyous occasion I had been picturing for the past two years. Rimpoche was lying on a bed in the next room, wrapped in his maroon robe. He did not turn his head or open his eyes, and occasionally a groan of pain escaped his lips. I sat by his bedside, exchanging remarks with the family about Rimpoche's condition. After a while there was nothing more to say, and I devoted myself to the silent repetition of the White Tārā mantra. Rimpoche had been delighted I was reciting it for Sangharakshita; now I was reciting it for him.

Over the next couple of days I spent much time around the school, trying not to impose on the family in their time of trouble. They, however, did not seem to see things in this way, and were very welcoming. Before I left, Jampel Kaldhen presented me, on behalf of Dhardo Rimpoche, with a photograph of one of Rimpoche's thangkas – of White Tārā – and with that plastic mala, which was one of several that Rimpoche had used during his recent pilgrimage to Nepal.

I hoped I might be able to return to Kalimpong if Rimpoche recovered, but unfortunately about a week later I heard that my father had died. I had to fly back to England at once.

So what was I left with from my communication and meeting with Rimpoche? I half expected to feel that the whole trip had been a disaster, in which after two years I finally turned up in Kalimpong, was unable to talk with Rimpoche, watched him suffering with a terrible headache, and emerged clasping some cheap plastic beads. Yet I have never had a sense that my journey was wasted, although I cannot fully articulate why. I gained a great deal from my contact with the Kaldhens. Not only were they very kind and hospitable to me at a time of great trouble, but their love and tremendous respect for Rimpoche made a strong impression on me, and indirectly increased my own feelings for him.

More than that, I had travelled several thousand miles in hope of a meeting with a smiling lama, and of being instructed in a new meditation practice. None of this had happened. Instead I had been presented with an opportunity to give, by chanting mantras at his bedside, and to receive nothing in return. This was itself a gift. The situation required that I let go of all my hopes and expectations and give myself up to what was happening. I had hoped to be bathed in Rimpoche's friendliness and to receive instruction in meditation. Instead I received some very clear teachings on impermanence, suffering, and the uselessness of mundane hopes and expectations.

Nothing special happened while I sat by that plain bed, next to that old man in his simple maroon robe. Yet somehow I left Kalimpong feeling that I had met Rimpoche, as the Kaldhen family had invited me to. In a way that I cannot fully account for, I came away with a strong sense of Rimpoche's kindness and wisdom. I also realized that my trip to Kalimpong had been a kind of pilgrimage, and that the point of pilgrimage is to travel the road with a faithful heart. If you do that you receive the benefits, even if the goal of your journey turns out to be cloud-hidden, whereabouts unknown.

Manjusvara

In March 1990, Meg Moginot and I were in India to celebrate our recent marriage as well as to work on another *Karuna Trust Newsletter*. I was writing copy and Meg was taking photographs. We arrived in Darjeeling heavy with the news that Dhardo Rimpoche was seriously ill. After telephoning Mahamati and Lokamitra back in Poona, we agreed to proceed to the school, making it clear to Jampel that on no account must we disturb Rimpoche. With some trepidation – for a number of Order members were already stranded in Darjeeling – Meg and I set off for Kalimpong. Although we spent two delightful days with the children at the school, all the time we were acutely aware that Dhardo Rimpoche lay just across the courtyard.

On our last evening at the school, as Meg and I were finishing our supper, Jampel came into our room and announced that Rimpoche wanted to see us. Supported by Meg, I explained our promise to Mahamati and Lokamitra that we would not disturb Rimpoche. But Jampel was adamant. He said, 'When Rimpoche asks to see you, you must go.' Clearly we had no choice. We followed Jampel across the courtyard and up the narrow stairs to Rimpoche's quarters. Rimpoche was lying in bed. In the corner of the candle-lit room stood Jampel's wife, who had been giving Rimpoche her constant attention. Rimpoche roused himself when he saw us and smiled. He said my name and then a few more words in Tibetan. Jampel explained that Rimpoche remembered my visit to the school the previous year. With a weak gesture of his arm Rimpoche ushered Meg and me to sit beside him.

My father had died just a few weeks previously. I remembered sitting with his corpse in the hospital morgue. Perhaps because of this I was unusually aware of the presence of death, for I was now sure that Rimpoche was dying. I looked across at Meg and knew she felt the same. What came to me was that Rimpoche wanted us somehow to witness, as it were, his leaving. Everyone at the school so loved Rimpoche that perhaps it was impossible for them to face the sad truth. This, at least, had been the impression that Meg and I had gradually been forming since our arrival the previous day.

After saying a few more words, Rimpoche slumped back and appeared to lose consciousness. I took his hand and was to continue holding it firmly for the next hour or so. I struggled to gather my thoughts. I was, I felt sure, at the deathbed of my teacher's teacher. What on earth should I do? Then, suddenly, feeling strangely calm, it became clear: I began to do the Green Tārā meditation practice that Sangharakshita had given me on my ordination at Guhyaloka in 1987.

What happened next is easier to write than explain. At some point I had a very strong sense of both Rimpoche and me momentarily leaving our bodies and rising up into the sky where we were embraced in the pure green radiance that surrounded Tārā. If this didn't unnerve me as much as it should it was because I had already left my body at least once before – after a car accident in San Francisco in 1981. Indeed I had discussed this incident with Rimpoche the previous year when he had asked me why I had become a Buddhist. He had responded that to have a strong sense of death is to have a strong Going for Refuge.

Eventually, Rimpoche regained consciousness. Meg and I prostrated before him and began to leave. But Rimpoche beckoned us back. He produced two malas that he proceeded to bless and give to us, and then some incense which he asked me to give to Sangharakshita. Sixteen days later, on 24 March, Dhardo Rimpoche died. Meg and I were the last members of the FWBO to see him alive.

Sinhadevi

In January 1990 I was a free woman. I had just turned down the offer of a secure and nearly satisfying career as a English teacher. I had carefully packed my bags, left my home, and bid my friends of long standing farewell. After nearly twenty years of hectic London life, I was stealing out of town alone.

A tantalizing choice lay before me. Should I follow the dictates of my heart, board a plane for India, and make my way up into the foothills of the Himalayas, up to the realm of a living Bodhisattva whose compassion had changed my life? Or should I follow the advice of spiritual friends and embark instead on a two-month solitary retreat, steeping myself in meditation in the depths of the English countryside? I finally chose the latter – and, in a certain respect, realized both.

I met Dhardo Rimpoche most memorably as we were both dying: he was dying in the physical sense, lying in a darkened room in Kalimpong; I was dying in the spiritual sense, sitting before him on a lonely, windswept night in Norfolk. He had been a constant guide throughout my two months of solitude, appearing in dreams, reflections, and meditations. His was a stern, uncompromising presence, always demanding my best; his was a kind and encouraging voice, and an almost unbearable tenderness wrapping itself around me. When I threw all my hopes to the ground and sat weeping in despair before my glowing shrine he was there, his eyes quizzical. I had come this far along the path to perfection, how could I give up now? How could I expect miracles to happen if I stood in the way?

Impermanence was the insistent theme of that retreat. Walking through the fields every day, the signs were everywhere: in the little heap of clean, white bones where, a night or so earlier, an owl had swooped on a shocked rabbit; in the darkening carcass of the lonely drake who had been swimming solitary only the morning before, snow white on the backwater while I silently watched and wondered. And most insistently, most vividly of all, that sense of impermanence was there in my nightly rituals of confession and resolve and in my spiritual struggles, when every inch of a move forward into a new and greater understanding meant leaving a little of the old me behind, dead as a doornail. I felt alternately like a ghost and an angel as I wandered the spreading fields at night, or as, unseen in the darkening lanes, I caught the sound of human voices drifting through cottage window panes. The chill of death ran through my veins, made me catch my breath at odd moments, woke me at night in paroxysms of fear and wonder. But every death brings a rebirth, and a vision of newness rose with the sun every morning, rippling happily through my awareness as I sat in meditation. I felt that Dhardo Rimpoche was expertly guiding me through the twisting labyrinth of dreams and dreads through which I was moving. His presence in my meditations calmed and focused my mind, his example filled my heart with light and faith. He led me onwards until I felt positively grasped in the heart of his greater existence. And when I emerged from that solitary retreat strong and confident and happy, moving calmly through this madly restless world, he was there too in my heart's core.…

Arriving in Norwich fresh from solitude I was shown into a friend's empty guest-room. In one corner was a shrine, dressed in richly coloured cloths, quietly glittering with jewels. It was dedicated to Dhardo Rimpoche, and I found myself sinking to my knees in reverence and gratitude. I meditated and performed puja, chanting the White Tārā mantra into the night. And then I began puja again, drawn irresistibly to prostrate before him, dedicating myself to my teacher's teacher. Strangely, a vivid vision of his life began to unfold unexpectedly before me. A succession of images of his life and work that I watched in quiet awe: his childhood in Dhartsendo, his monastery training, his illnesses, his victories, his work in Bodh Gaya, his dedication to the ITBCI School that was so dear to his heart. All I knew or had ever heard about him took form in that stream of images that engulfed me in its quality of purity and purpose. And now here he was, more present than ever before, the significance of his life overwhelming me, stars in the sky dancing with joy at his being, celebrating his life, witnessing my gratitude to him overflowing in an unstoppable and unthinking flood of tears. Had I made the right choice in withdrawing into solitude, in turning away from the opportunity of meeting him face to face?

The next morning I met Srimala. As I leaned back into her sofa ready to tell her about my retreat, she asked me if I had heard the news. The news? About Dhardo Rimpoche. I had heard no news at all for over two months. He died last night, she said quietly.

Teeth are the most visible sign of our skeleton, our friendly reminders of death. Rimpoche used to chant mantras under his breath as he brushed his teeth in the morning. I often think of him as I brush mine, imagining his image with the glowing form of White Tārā (one of his main visualization practices) just above, her mantra softly circling him while he invokes her, silently, all the while polishing those visible reminders. White Tārā, the Radiant One of Long Life, her mantra echoing through time and space, through life and death, connecting the Greatly Precious One of Dhartsendo with his spiritual sons and daughters in all corners of this slowly revolving Earth.

Maitreyi

The stupa rises from a grassy mound, the red sandstone dappled with sunlight shining through the overhanging branches of a tall ash tree. It looks as though it has always been there, not so much ancient as timeless; a part of the landscape as much as the trees and hills, yet emanating a different presence. From the retreat centre I can read part of the inscription carved around the base and embellished with gold leaf. Shining out the letters read 'Radiate love.'

The stupa contains some of the ashes of Dhardo Rimpoche, teacher and friend to Sangharakshita and regarded by him as a Bodhisattva. For many years now I have been affected by hearing about Rimpoche; hearing about his life dedicated to the Dharma, hearing the accounts of friends who met him and carry with them the memory of his kindness, seeing his photograph, now a familiar feature of many personal shrines.

My own 'meeting' with Dhardo Rimpoche took place over the eighteen months during which I oversaw the building of the stupa at Tiratanaloka, the retreat centre where I live and work. I was much inspired by the vision of the project but somewhat daunted by what it involved. At the outset, the practical aspects preoccupied me greatly and were the cause of considerable anxiety: which stone to use? what site to choose? who would do the work?… But what I became increasingly aware of was another dimension that was emerging; a field of beneficial activity generated by the vision of the stupa, a gathering momentum within which the practical details fell into place and into perspective.

The vision of the stupa captured people's imagination as the life and person of Rimpoche had captured their hearts. So many people were not only willing but evidently happy to give money, time, and energy to the project. To be on the receiving end of so much generosity was a very joyful experience. Amid the generosity emerged a web of individual but interconnected efforts; Rod Drew was carving the stone in Cambridge, in the Windhorse Trading warehouse, supported to do so by the business – and therefore by the work of all those in the shops, on the vans, and in the offices. In East London Chintamani was casting the gold finial of the space and consciousness elements; in the garden at Tiratanaloka Ingrid and fellow workers were shifting a huge heap of earth to create the stupa mound and garden. In West London Naseem and Hannah were devising a fund-raising venture, 'Miraculous Mind', in which people all around the world participated. Offerings arrived from many places to be placed in and around the stupa; flags from Kalimpong, small objects of devotion, a beautiful hand-made book from Glasgow inscribed with Dharmic verses and rejoicings in Dhardo Rimpoche. The second part of Dhardo Rimpoche's message, 'Live united,' was being enacted all around me as the cooperation and interconnected efforts of all these people brought the stupa into being, made the vision into reality.

Dhardo Rimpoche's message and his presence began to enter our lives at Tiratanaloka more and more strongly as the project neared completion and the erection of the stupa began on the lawn in front of the retreat centre. As the day arrived on which Sangharakshita was to dedicate the stupa by placing within it a portion of the ashes, I became vividly aware that Tiratanaloka would not be the same place once the ceremony had been performed, and that I would not be the same person, because my life would be being lived in the presence of a Bodhisattva. Sangharakshita's words on that day were confirmation of this intimation, 'One could say that you now have Dhardo Rimpoche there, in the stupa, or represented by the stupa, witnessing not just the day-to-day life of Tiratanaloka but especially witnessing people's Going for Refuge. Witnessing the performance of that miracle of transformation of life that takes place when someone goes for Refuge to the Three Jewels.'

I see the stupa, circumambulating it through the changing seasons, set against the fiery colours of autumn and now the bare branches of winter. A kind of energy radiates from it, the eye is drawn towards it, and each time I see it my heart lifts. It is a deep red-brown after rain, a soft pink in the sunshine, witnessing the life of Tiratanaloka and shining out its message; the message of Dhardo Rimpoche, 'Cherish the Doctrine, live united, radiate love.'

Danavira

I never met Dhardo Rimpoche. I have only ever seen pictures of him. All I know about him I heard from others. Those who have sat in his company reported back on the pleasure of that experience. All who heard from these witnesses concluded, with the witnesses themselves, that Dhardo Rimpoche was a true follower of the Buddha. In a fallible world, he was a cause for rejoicing.

I accept now that all our lives are lived in interconnection. We exist as part of a great, deep net of being, where every smile or tear becomes us all, as if each were the only eyes of the ocean, the sea itself the lives of others. Thus personalized, in our blood, is the breath of nominal strangers. Their actions also make the waves and spray of being we call our own. All partake of each other. Everything, everywhere, done now, in a true web of life, which rumbles in our hearts, is perceived by us individually as the thunder of our immanence. So that the wise take profound steps only, knowing that they walk for us all, to keep us from harm.

I know little of Dhardo Rimpoche's life. I do know that during one of the more violent periods of the twentieth century, when some of the worst sides of our common human nature roamed, bestial and freed, across the world, he and others like him had the favourable conditions to study the Dharma of wisdom and compassion. Who but the Buddhas could measure the depths of such lives, lived humanely in brutal times, or mark their impact upon the force of history? All this was before I was born. Yet this stream of consciousness I call myself, I count as eased in that time, from the grip of that vast catastrophe, by the actions and mind of such a one as Dhardo Rimpoche. Later, from the ashes of his own Tibetan world, he built a school for refugees and the children of the poor. All that he had he gave to others, status and position he put aside, a son of the Buddha, replete with the generosity of a wealthy heart. Mothers and fathers biologically produce us and bring us up but only the wise are truly parents to our minds. Though I never met Dhardo Rimpoche, I think of him as a spiritual father.

It is my Buddhist practice now to dedicate each day and night to the Three Jewels. By this means I hope to orientate my wayward self, align it with the Truth, in rising into common wakefulness or sinking into sleep. Thus I make a lighthouse for my heart so that it will seek what is true across the ill-lit ocean of being, a clear path, in the welter of the world's conditioning, towards nirvāṇa. For my imperfect mind the difference between being from the drowned or the saved forms a contrast from which I strive. As such, when sensible, I cling to anything offering the hope of Emancipation. These are my compass marks for day or night.

All the Buddhas, the Dharma Truths, but especially the Sangha, I invoke to aid and guide me. Sangharakshita, my own preceptor, whose prosperous mind revealed my limitations and made my roof the sky, I call upon daily in spiritual practice.

Then to the Dharma deeps I cast my moments and to their timeless lives I turn my temporal mind for contact with great Buddhists. In my case Longchenpa, Hui-Neng, Han Shan, Tilopa, Nagarjuna, Padmasambhava, and then, of course, Dhardo Rimpoche; finally to Siddhartha Gautama, the Buddha.

Such minds as these I call upon to influence my mind beyond the limitations of our blind history. Their every action ripples still throughout our present streets. Yet we numb ourselves to them, thinking them dead and gone, after all, and make a barrier of our ignorance to their wisdom, as if the Awakened Mind dissolved or disappeared, or fell asleep again, across the great net of being and interpenetration. It is my mind that sleeps and wilfully obscures my sight of the Buddha. Are you like me? I prefer a harder life, in the grim vestiges of the flesh, in flames, of a burning known — against release in cool nirvāṇa. This is a fool's cosmos. Twice a day I remind myself that the view it takes on space and time is false, and that great Buddhists abound, and of how we live in our entirety in the instant of their compassion.

Though I never met Dhardo Rimpoche, he is such a one, worthy of remembrance, on the evidence of his life, in the presence of his reality.

from Kalimpong

Mahamati

Mahamati, a member of the Western Buddhist Order, has been associated with the ITBCI School since 1985. He has visited the school regularly since 1994 and is now one of its trustees.

I had been due to meet Dhardo Rimpoche for the first time on 21 March 1990, but, knowing of his illness and not wishing to trouble him or those looking after him, I cancelled my travel arrangements. So it was not until 1994 that I finally visited the ITBCI School. Since then I have returned several times and I feel that, although I was not destined to meet Rimpoche in the flesh, I have come to know him through others who had been very close to him, and also simply through taking in the atmosphere of the school itself.

Arriving at the school for the first time in May 1994 I didn't have any sense of disappointment that Rimpoche was not there. On the contrary, through the welcome that I received from the Kaldhen family and simply from just being there, I felt myself propelled into some kind of higher state of consciousness. It's something quite difficult to explain, but it's an experience that has returned to me again and again whilst visiting the school, and I can only sum it up by saying that the ITBCI School is a very special place for me.

I was very fortunate to be asked by Sara Hagel, of Windhorse Publications, to conduct some interviews in Kalimpong for this tenth anniversary publication. From those interviews I came to understand more fully – as I hope you will too – how it is that the spirit of Dhardo Rimpoche lives on in those who were close to him, and still feel close to him today.

I was struck by how easy I found it to conduct the interviews – because all those I spoke to knew exactly what they wanted to say. I jotted down notes as the interviews proceeded and typed them up soon afterwards, usually in the same sequence and missing out very little, if anything. Jampel Kaldhen, his daughter Zenden, and his son Jigme spoke to me in English; the others were mediated by Jampel's translation, and for Yankyidla and Tsering Wangdi by Zenden's. Sometimes I prompted with a question, but sometimes, as for example with Mrs Kaldhen, I just listened as the memories unfolded. Afterwards Mrs Kaldhen said that she was very happy that she had been able to express whatever she wanted to say. I hope that all those interviewed would feel likewise, although I couldn't help thinking that there must still be a wealth of untapped memories about Rimpoche, both from those represented in these interviews and from others whom I was unable to meet.

I found it remarkable that all those I spoke to came back again and again to Rimpoche's outstanding qualities of kindness and generosity. They had themselves been recipients of his kindness and generosity, and had at the same time been inspired to practise those qualities in their own lives. It is this spirit of Dhardo Rimpoche that lives on today at the school and among all those who have been profoundly affected by him, and which I believe accounts for the very special atmosphere one finds there. In a sense, through these interviews I had the good fortune to come into contact with Rimpoche himself, and I hope that through reading them you too will have that same good fortune.

Mr Jampel Kaldhen

Jampel Kaldhen came to Kalimpong from Rimpoche's estate in Tibet in 1956. He became Rimpoche's secretary and headmaster of the ITBCI School. In his will Dhardo Rimpoche described Jampel as his 'beloved adopted son'.

I completed my Tibetan education syllabus in Lhasa in 1956 at the early age of ten. My father had been the manager of Rimpoche's estate in Lhasa, Thonga-sheka, until his death in 1955, and before that my grandfather, who had been the cousin of the first Dhardo Tulku, had been manager. After my father died my sister took over the management of the estate.

My family often wrote to Rimpoche asking him to return to Tibet as he had not visited since 1951, and likewise the monks and servants in Rimpoche's Labhrang at Drepung. In 1956 Rimpoche wrote a letter saying, 'for the time being I will not come, but instead you should send the two boys because they have completed their education.' Those two boys were my elder brother and me. Rimpoche told me later on that actually he knew that China would invade Tibet, and that he as well as my brother and I would never return, but he didn't want to say so in case they wouldn't send us.

My sister's husband arranged to send us in the company of a big officer's son who was travelling in a van across the mountains from Lhasa to Sikkim. When we arrived at the border we came across the Karmapa, along with his huge retinue, who was also coming to India. The officer's son was known by the Karmapa, he provided us with horses, and we reached Gangtok as part of the Karmapa's retinue to be treated as honoured guests. We enjoyed this welcome for about three days. At that time Rimpoche had come to Gangtok to meet the Chogyal (King of Sikkim) to discuss with him the Dalai Lama's visit to India in a couple of months' time for the Buddha's 2,500th Jayanti.

Then my brother and I were taken by jeep to Kalimpong, where we were joined by Rimpoche three days later.

I could recite many things from school, and Rimpoche was very pleased. I spoke little and did whatever I was told. After a couple of months Rimpoche asked me to teach the small children, even though I was only ten. For one or two years I taught class one.

In 1959 Rimpoche engaged a monk very well versed in Tibetan grammar to give lessons at the school. This monk told Rimpoche that I was very good at Tibetan and I should write a modern grammar book. I already knew some English grammar because I'd had a very rigorous teaching from Bhante Sangharakshita for two years. Rimpoche encouraged me to write the grammar book and at the age of thirteen I completed it. Rimpoche bought a hand-operated duplicating machine, and lots of stencils and paper. I wrote the book on the stencils and published copies. The grammar book became popular and was used in several schools in Kalimpong as well as our own. Then Rimpoche suggested I write a book on spelling, so I did that too and we published it on the duplicator.

Later on, after I had become a teacher, Rimpoche asked me to compile a series of textbooks. Rimpoche told me to make them as lively as possible. He told me to choose stories with a moral lesson and some link with Buddhism. Rimpoche liked the books very much and they are still used in schools. Rimpoche also asked me to publish His Holiness the Dalai Lama's *The Future Constitution of Tibet*, because it was very important. At that time it had not been published, but Rimpoche had collected extracts as they had appeared locally in a Tibetan newspaper published in Darjeeling. At the end of this book, after the Dalai Lama's writings, we placed a song composed by Rimpoche called 'The Song of 1959'. Roughly translated from the Tibetan it runs:

Hailstorms fall heavily from clouds in the East,
But they cannot destroy the barrier of the West.
Though the cloud in the East is dark and forceful,
It won't last for long.

It will be driven out by the Wind of Truth.
The peaceful wind will drive out the dark red cloud;
The seed of Freedom will ripen in due course.
As it is said, if crops are spoiled by hailstorm,
Next year there will be so much crop that we will
Need to build a new granary.
The powerful, supreme knowledge will be greater than before.
As the sun rises, and warms the earth without discrimination,
Likewise the Dalai Lama is the Protector of all beings.
As the rain showers from the sky and moistens the earth without discrimination,
Likewise the Dalai Lama is the Protector of all beings.
As the water of the oceans is used by all beings,
Likewise the Dalai Lama is the Protector of all beings.
As many trees and bushes grow in this great Earth,
Likewise the Dalai Lama is the Protector of all beings.

We have performed this song as a *khampa*, or folk dance, many times.

Rimpoche was very fond of Tibetan culture. He knew there was no Tibetan musical notation for secular music, although there is notation for religious music. He had a very, very deep concern about this. People used to learn the notation in Chinese sounds and Rimpoche didn't like this. He said we should have our own. I read a lot of books on Western and Indian music. I have still not completed this project though I am determined to do so. I feel a little regret that due to my responsibilities as headmaster of the school I could not complete this work during Rimpoche's lifetime. The book is half complete and I hope I can complete it and print a few copies on the occasion of Rimpoche's tenth death anniversary.

In 1978 I had an offer of a good job in Delhi as a translator. I went to Rimpoche to ask him for his advice. Rimpoche said, 'Look, I don't want to say don't go, but just listen carefully to this Tibetan proverb: Even if the dog's tail is thick and hairy, it can only cover its own nose.' He meant to say, 'OK, if you go there you may get a good post and a good salary, but the benefit will be limited.' He compared the dog's nose to my own benefit. So I told the person who had offered me the job, 'No, I have to obey my guru.'

Subsequently Rimpoche used the same proverb many times when advising me. One such occasion was in 1986. I had been a teacher in a government high school in Kalimpong since 1978. I used to teach in the ITBCI School every day before and after my government job. Rimpoche quoted the same proverb and said, 'At the government high school you have a handsome salary and are safe and sound for the future, but now I am quite old, and if you take the responsibility for the running of this school you can serve your own people and give greater service for your culture.' Then I resigned from the high school and came to work full-time at the ITBCI School. Rimpoche was so pleased, but many of my old colleagues thought I was wasting my knowledge serving in a small school, just as many people used to say and think of Rimpoche that he was wasting his time in a small school instead of looking after a big monastery. Rimpoche often told my wife and me, 'Just concentrate on this school. It is more significant than you think.'

Rimpoche had a monk assistant called Kusho Solponpa (Venerable Losang Namkha) who for many years used to make the daily *tormas* (offerings) for Rimpoche. After he died, in 1984, Rimpoche made them himself for a couple of months, and then taught me how to make them. So since 1985 until Rimpoche's death I made the offerings for Rimpoche every day after work. One torma had to be made every day, and at the end of the Tibetan month a whole trayful. I would arrange everything on the shrine. Rimpoche was very particular about how it should all be done. If the size was even slightly wrong he would be very upset. And making the offering must never be hurried, even though I became skilled and could do it very quickly.

Rimpoche did not like to use inferior *tsampa* for the offerings. He said that any offering should be made only with the best quality materials. Previously in Kalimpong people made *tshog* with more water and less butter, but because of Rimpoche's constant teaching regarding how to offer *tshog* people now put seven parts butter with one part water.

Every tenth and twenty-fifth of the Tibetan month, Rimpoche brought bread and sweets and offered *tshog* to Vajrayogini. According to the Vajrayogini practice the *tshog* is to be given only to young girls, so at that time the girls in the hostel were very happy!

Rimpoche used to say it is very good to receive initiations as a blessing. However, if you can't do the necessary obligations it would be better not to receive it. He explained that these practices came from the Tantra, and if we practise them it will have a fruitful effect, but if we don't practise it will be harmful. He explained the difference between sūtra and tantra. As regards sūtra the more that you can hear the better, but tantra involves meditation with visualization and recitation, and once we receive an initiation we have an obligation to practise it every day. He also explained that whoever gives you the initiation you should henceforth treat as your guru. Even if they act like a dog you must still keep strong faith in them as your guru. Because of Rimpoche's advice I have received very few initiations from him, only whatever I could actually practise. When other Rimpoches visited I would go along for a brief audience and a blessing but I would not take any initiations from them. This is not out of lack of faith in these other Rimpoches but because I knew that I could not undertake any further obligations.

At the end of 1989, three weeks before leaving for Kathmandu, Rimpoche called me one day and asked me to draft a resolution to the State Bank of India so that instead of only himself as cheque signatory, which previously had been the case, either of us could sign. I said to Rimpoche, 'Forget it. After coming back from Nepal we will do this.' But he insisted, 'No, no, do it now.' The day after we returned from Nepal Rimpoche became very sick, so if he had not insisted on making me a signatory there would have been many problems as he then became too ill to sign his name.

I was very, very close to Rimpoche, and when he was sick he was always saying 'Anu, Anu,' as he used to call me. But actually he depended more on my wife, because he said that I was not forceful enough and he thought my wife was stronger.

Mrs N.C. Kaldhen

Mrs Kaldhen came to Kalimpong as a refugee in 1959 and met Dhardo Rimpoche when she attended the ITBCI School. She eventually married Jampel and had four children. She acted as Rimpoche's attendant in his last years.

I first met Rimpoche at the age of thirteen, soon after I had arrived as a refugee from Tibet in 1959. My cousin and I went with our elders to the Himalayan Hotel in Kalimpong to cut grass. The hotel was owned by a fat English lady whose name I don't remember, and she said that such small children shouldn't be doing that kind of work. She said that there was a small school run by a lama and it would be better if I went there. She gave me a letter of introduction to Rimpoche, I approached him, and he said that I could start at his school the following day. After a few months I was selected as a boarder.

On Saturdays and Sundays Rimpoche used to take the hostel children to the school and teach us sewing in order to make school badges, which he had designed himself. On those days Rimpoche would give us big glasses of tea and bread that he purchased from a roadside hawker, so we loved to do that work. When we arrived in India we had no proper bedding but Rimpoche gave us new blankets for sleeping and clothes for school. I stayed in the hostel for almost three years until the government stopped the grant. Many children had to leave, but Rimpoche kept me with him.

My uncle talked with Rimpoche about my marriage when I was sixteen. I felt very, very sad. I cried and said that I would jump in the Teesta River. The ladies hugged me and told me not to do this. Actually I was so ignorant I didn't even know where the Teesta was.

I was married to one of Rimpoche's servants, Tenzing-la, who was aged around thirty-five. I had no interest in marrying but my uncle said that if I married I would be living with a Rimpoche so I would be cared for. After two years Tenzing-la died. At that time I was bearing a child. When the baby was born I didn't know how to look after her. Rimpoche named her Pelkhar Lhamo. I was living in the Labhrang with Rimpoche. Because I had no husband Rimpoche looked after me and also helped look after my child. After about one year the baby had a fall from a height and died in hospital. Rimpoche came to the hospital and took the dead body and brought the baby to the school. Rimpoche said 'You shouldn't worry, this is a karmic fruit, nobody can help it.'

When I went to the bazaar I felt quite awkward as everyone was staring at me because I had lost my husband and then my child. I felt quite dark and depressed. One day I told Rimpoche how I was feeling. Rimpoche said, 'Everyone in the world wants good things and good fortune, but whatever happens to you, you must bear it because it is karmic consequence.' Even so I felt depressed and became very weak.

After one year I married Anu-la (Jampel Kaldhen) who was the son of Rimpoche's previous manager in Tibet. I don't know how it came about that he was ready to marry me because at that time Anu-la was very proud and he was an educated person, unlike me. It must have been Rimpoche's blessings and also there may have been a karmic connection between us.

After that I became the cook for the hostel children and also the school caretaker. At that time we had very little money so I had to do everything for the hostel children myself, including washing and stitching their clothes. At the same time I was bringing up four children.

Rimpoche was very kind to all my children. From very young Zenden always wanted to sleep near to Rimpoche. Rimpoche did more for my children than even a parent could have done. Then in 1984 Rimpoche's close attendant died and I had to cook for Rimpoche and take care of him, and someone else cooked for the hostel. And twice a year I would accompany Rimpoche to Ghoom.

By experiencing how Rimpoche used to care for others I felt that I also should try to become a quite extraordinary person. I was not able to change myself to such an extent, but Rimpoche's example brought about changes in me. Rimpoche always used to tell me, 'You must look after the hostel children as though they were your own. If you do this it is not necessary to cut your hair, wear robes, and become a nun.' I could not fulfil even half of whatever Rimpoche said, but according to my capacity I remembered Rimpoche's advice about the orphans. Even today I try to treat those orphans like my own children.

Regarding Rimpoche's kindness and love I cannot express what I feel. I remember it more and more since he died. My feeling to help others is stronger and stronger, but due to my ill health I cannot work as before. Whenever I have a good day I think it is because of the blessings of Rimpoche and Bhante Sangharakshita and all our members [the FWBO]. I can never, ever forget this. I hope that the chain started by the strong connection between Rimpoche and Bhante Sangharakshita will go on for ever so as to spread the Dharma wider and wider. I hope that the new Rimpoche will fulfil the work of Dhardo Rimpoche.

Mr Tashi Dorje

Mr Tashi Dorje was teacher of Tibetan language at the ITBCI School from the founding of the school until his retirement in 1996. He first met Rimpoche in 1949, when he was a travelling businessman, soon after Rimpoche arrived in Kalimpong.

I was very attracted to Rimpoche from the first meeting. In Tibet I had met many other Rimpoches but I felt an instant attraction to Dhardo Rimpoche. He looked like a simple monk, and spoke very calmly and directly. I remember on that first occasion he spoke of the importance of being kind to all beings.

Over the next few years many Rimpoches came from Tibet. Many of the big Rimpoches would only respond to those who were wealthy or powerful. But our Rimpoche was ready to go anywhere. There was a place called Banglang where the beggars slept. Whenever one of the beggars was sick or had died Rimpoche would go. He wasn't concerned for himself, he cared for the common people – that's why he established our school.

Due to my contact with Rimpoche I became a teacher at his school and I had everything that I could wish for. Of course the pay was very limited, but I felt that it was good to work with Rimpoche. I worked for the school as if it was my own family, because of Rimpoche. I used to supplement my income by writing letters for businessmen, and my wife worked. When I was a businessman there were a lot of ups and downs in my life. But after I received Rimpoche's blessings everything in my life went smoothly.

For blessings to be effective two important factors are required. Firstly I had a great deal of faith in Rimpoche, and secondly Rimpoche had a very strong feeling for me. I also feel that there must have been a previous karmic connection. But it is very difficult to know how it was that we came together here in India and felt such a strong connection.

Rimpoche gave me a job and in that sense was my master, but in another way he was my root guru and gave me many initiations and empowerments. So although Rimpoche's physical presence is no longer here I still feel for him very strongly as my root guru and pray to him every day.

On one occasion my second son, Tshering Palden, was seriously ill with a mental sickness. I went to see the oracle who told me that I needed a particular blessing and empowerment that was very rare. Rimpoche agreed to give this to me, and very soon my son was completely cured.

I remember very well Rimpoche's last teaching in Kalimpong Town Hall, which lasted twenty-nine days. This was in November 1989. During that time Rimpoche explained many things very simply and clearly and gave many empowerments and initiations. Some Rimpoches are scholars, some are well-versed in teaching, some have a deep practice. Our Rimpoche was a scholar and well versed in teaching, and he also had a deep practice which materialized in daily life. For this reason I feel he was a Bodhisattva. He was very kind and loving towards beings, very broad-minded and tolerant. At the same time he did whatever he thought was correct, whatever others might say.

During Rimpoche's life I had a number of significant dreams. I had one dream in December 1989 during Rimpoche's pilgrimage to Nepal. At the time, I was in Gangtok visiting my son. The dream was set in Tibet, at Ganden Monastery. A large assembly of monks was performing an important puja, and Rimpoche was there to lead it. On Rimpoche's head was a crown bearing the emblem of the five Buddhas. Many people placed flags surrounding the monastery. At first I felt this was a good sign, but then I found myself arriving at the school and saw many monks doing puja. The place seemed very dark and sad. Then I met Jampel-la and he too seemed very sad and about to cry.

After a few days I heard that Rimpoche was sick. And when I returned to the school I saw the same thing I had seen in the dream. Shortly before Rimpoche was reborn I had many dreams. They showed me the strong blessings of Rimpoche, and the strong faith in him that I have always felt.

Mrs T. Wangdi

Mrs T. Wangdi first heard about Rimpoche in 1949. In that year Rimpoche had taken up a new responsibility as abbot of the Tibetan temple in Bodh Gaya, and each year would retreat from the summer heat to Kalimpong.

In 1949 I had four young children to look after and a fifth on its way. I was too busy to go to Tirpai on the outskirts of Kalimpong, where Rimpoche had taken up residence with his mother, but my mother and mother-in-law and many other ladies used to go there regularly, and when they came back I heard them talk about the young Rimpoche they had visited. They were very impressed by the Rimpoche who was so young and gave such good sermons.

In 1951 my husband became seriously ill. A famous doctor in Calcutta said that he had a malignant tumour in his stomach and unless this was operated on immediately he would die. My mother-in-law said that first she must visit Rimpoche and seek his advice. Rimpoche was concerned because at that time my husband, who was quite a bit older than me, was in his forty-ninth year, which is an inauspicious year according to Tibetans. Rimpoche performed a *mo*,[*] and told my mother-in-law that 'on no account should a knife be put into your son's body'. He told us to have certain pujas done to remove obstacles to my husband's life, and these we sponsored at the monastery in Ghoom. My mother-in-law had a great deal of faith in Rimpoche, and I accepted his advice. We went instead to a homoeopathic doctor in Darjeeling who gave my husband some pills and put him on some dietary restrictions. Soon afterwards my husband, who was a lawyer and public prosecutor, stood for the state elections, canvassing in Siliguri and Kurseoing. My husband was still in considerable pain and

---

A prediction involving the invocation of a particular deity and the throwing of dice. See *The Wheel and the Diamond*, op.cit., p.80.

sometimes when people demanded to see the candidate it wasn't possible because he was too sick. Even so, he won the election and we moved to Calcutta where my husband was a minister for the next fifteen years. He gradually recovered from his illness.

After that, whenever something happened I used to run to Rimpoche. Whenever my children and then grandchildren reached an inauspicious year I would ask Rimpoche for an amulet. It was not a small thing for Rimpoche to give an amulet. He would ask for details of the person and then ask me to return after a few days. He would perform certain rituals, and when I returned he would give me the amulet, which I would place on my child in order to drive away evil spirits.

In 1957 there was another election and I went to Rimpoche requesting protection for my husband against obstructions, which he provided. And after that I visited Rimpoche at the time of every election until my husband retired from politics.

In 1984, when my husband was dying, by good fortune Rimpoche was next door addressing the Tibetan Women's Association. He came immediately, and although my husband was no longer conscious he spoke to him on how to leave this life and go to the next, and recited prayers for his good rebirth. All my children were present at the bed-side, we chanted the mantra *oṁ maṇi padme hūṁ*, and I felt at peace.

After five months my second son, who was a helicopter pilot, was killed in a crash. Rimpoche asked for some of my son's clothing so that he could do puja for him. At that very difficult and sad time he visited me and he gave me courage.

After my husband's death I used to go next door to Sandhutsang Building on full moon and new moon days to listen to Rimpoche's sermons to the Tibetan Women's Association. His speeches were in simple Tibetan, which all the old ladies could understand. They would start at 2 o'clock and last an hour, and after that we used to offer him a khata, a little money, or any gift, as is our custom. Other Rimpoches came and went but our Rimpoche was here to give us permanent guidance. I have lived a long life and suffered a lot, and now my children have all gone their own ways. When the time comes for me to die I shall have no regrets.

Mr Tenzing Amdo

Mr Tenzing Amdo first met Rimpoche in 1961, two years after fleeing Tibet. He was then twenty-eight years old. He has served the ITBCI School as art teacher from then right up to the present day.

I strongly believe that our school has survived and developed because of Rimpoche's blessings and for no other reason. For many years the school received no outside financial support, but it survived because of Rimpoche's contact with well-wishers and because of his blessings. Rimpoche cared for the children, looking after them himself. He wouldn't call a doctor for minor illnesses, but treated the children himself. For many years he administered injections. (He was very particular about sterilizing the syringes by boiling them – not for a few minutes but for half an hour – and he would never allow anyone else to do it.) He never scolded or beat the children, but even so the children were quite scared of him because of his big personality.

During my time at the school I have seen many students and teachers come and go. In all those years I never experienced any disharmony, and I firmly believe that this is the blessing of Rimpoche. The most extraordinary thing of all was that Rimpoche would never refuse help to anyone. Whether approached for blessings in times of illness, death, or any other circumstance, Rimpoche would help all without distinction. It made no difference whether they were rich or poor. He would perform pujas anywhere for anyone, and up to the age of sixty-five he would travel anywhere to do it, often refusing transport and going on foot. After ariving here from Nepal Rimpoche fell sick and just wore blankets. I pleaded with Rimpoche 'Please wear your robes.' He said to me, 'I have worn my robes all my life. Now there is no need. Please put them away.' I couldn't understand this, but now I realize he knew he was dying. I could have put important questions to him then, but in my ignorance I failed to do so.

Mr Dogah

Mr Dogah was a pupil at the ITBCI School, where he was encouraged by Rimpoche to study Tibetan music and culture. He is now the dance and music teacher at the school.

In 1959, when I was fifteen years old, I came to Kalimpong as a refugee from Tibet. I came with my Jin-dag ('feudal master') and left my parents behind in Tibet. My Jin-dag told me there was a good school I should attend, and that turned out to be Rimpoche's school. At that time the school was run on traditional Tibetan lines in the Tibetan language only. In Tibet I had been a novice monk in a monastery, so this was my first experience of school. After a few months the school started teaching English and Hindi, and the children were asked to contribute one rupee a month, which my Jin-dag agreed to pay. In 1960, with funding from the government, I got the chance to be one of the first boarders at the school, but after two years the funding stopped. Some of the small children were sent to a new Tibetan Central School in another part of India, but about eight of the older boys like me were asked to go to work in a steel factory. We refused to go, and asked Rimpoche to allow us to work part-time so that we could continue our studies. We started making Tibetan boots and other things we could sell, and with this we were able to maintain the hostel for the remaining boys.

After a further year many of the older boys dispersed to different places, and my Jin-dag suggested he take me to Dalhousie. Rimpoche said he wasn't sure about that because of my poor health. I had come from Tibet with some sort of tuberculosis. He carried out a *mo* and said 'It would be better to stay in the school rather than go to Dalhousie.' Then another of my Jin-dags suggested sending me to Vellore in South India for medical treatment. Again Rimpoche did a *mo* and again said 'Don't go.'

Because of my constant illness I was unable to continue my studies, but I had a natural gift with my hands and I used this to make masks. In 1963 I made my first snow-lion mask using newspaper, old cloths, and anything else to hand. People had never seen such a thing before and it was really appreciated. Rimpoche told me what I had done was good and that gradually I could improve the quality. Next year Rimpoche organized our first cultural programme on School Day (the school's anniversary on 10 December), and in that year my illness completely disappeared.

Rimpoche was very fond of Tibetan culture, and along with prayers he collected Tibetan songs. He copied these out in his own hand and got the children to sing them after prayers. Some of the songs were written by big lamas, and Rimpoche would say, 'Don't think they are just songs. They are also prayers.'

Rimpoche sent two of us to a Tibetan musician to learn the lute and the dulcimer. My friend was unable to learn, but I did well. Rimpoche called some tailors to make traditional Tibetan dresses and Rimpoche himself made the ornaments, which was a very difficult job. Real ornaments were very costly, so Rimpoche asked some ladies to lend him their gold and silver ornaments, and he copied these to make artificial ornaments by filing down pieces of wood and plastic. We still have many of those ornaments that Rimpoche made, which I keep in good repair as I feel that they are special. Rimpoche was always very interested in cultural activities, and would ask artists visiting Kalimpong to perform at the school – and that's how I gained much of my experience.

Rimpoche often used to tell those who took part in the cultural programmes, 'Don't think this is just a show. Don't think this is ordinary culture. Our culture is linked with religion, so it is your duty to preserve it and pass it on to younger people.'

In about 1967 or 1968 a big officer from the Tibetan government in Dharamsala, who had been one of our family friends in Tibet, visited Kalimpong. He asked me, 'Why do you stay here? You are young and talented. If you come to Dharamsala you may even get the chance to go abroad.' I consulted Rimpoche. With a big smile he said, 'You are a very simple and straightforward person. If you go I don't think you will do more for the Tibetan cause. If you stay here I think you will do much, much more.'

In those days I received only fifteen rupees pocket money a month, but it never worried me as I had faith in Rimpoche. In 1976, when I was 31, Rimpoche advised me to get married. Then he threw a *mo* to find me a suitable wife, and advised me to marry a girl who had previously stayed in our hostel. Neither of us had much money but we got married and lived together in the hostel. Rimpoche often used to quote a Tibetan proverb, which translates something like: 'If you care for others, there is no need to care for yourself.' I feel this was true, because everything I wanted I have now achieved.

I often travelled with Rimpoche to the remote villages surrounding Kalimpong, travelling on foot up steep and rocky mountains, or through paddy fields deep in water. Sometimes I would plead with Rimpoche not to go, but he would say, 'These people came to seek some favour in time of difficulty. They have a lot of hope, so we mustn't refuse. This is the essence of Dharma. We must fulfil their hopes as far as we can.' Most of the village people who invited Rimpoche were Bhutanese and Sikkimese, and their monks were Kagyupa and Nyingmapa, not Gelugpa as Rimpoche was. But Rimpoche had no hesitation at all in joining them for their rituals. Some of them drank wine and chang and ate a lot of meat as part of their ritual, but Rimpoche wasn't bothered about this at all. If I had been Rimpoche I couldn't have tolerated it. In their hearts these monks were very, very faithful towards Rimpoche, but they had no idea how to receive a high lama. They treated him just like an ordinary monk. But this was only through their ignorance and it didn't bother Rimpoche. Sometimes we had to travel very long distances, on foot or in the back of a truck, sometimes not returning home until late at night. I often asked Rimpoche not to go, but he always went!

We Tibetans never ask a Rimpoche to sit all night by a dead body to perform puja; we ask the ordinary monks to do that. Out of ignorance the village people used to insist that our Rimpoche spent the whole night by the body, and he would stay and meditate and pray. The place would be very dirty and there would be no place to sleep.

Sometimes I got annoyed. I would tell Rimpoche 'You are such a learned person from such a great monastery, but they treat you like an ordinary monk.' Rimpoche would say, 'Just forget it. As long as what they wish for is fulfilled, then that's OK.'

Sometimes people used to backbite about Rimpoche. Later on they would regret it and come to Rimpoche for some favour. For Rimpoche there was no distinction between a very close disciple and those people who had abused him. He was ready to help all without making any distinction.

Zenden Lhamo

Zenden is the eldest child of Jampel and Mrs N.C. Kaldhen. She was born in June 1967. She is married with two children.

If ever I am afraid I think of our Rimpoche. He is everything to me. Even today I don't feel he has expired. Every day I pray to him to help me. I just talk to him: 'I am going to do this, or that, what do you think?' He has been a great influence on me. I always have his photograph with me. And wherever I live I have a shrine on which I put Rimpoche-la's photograph in the middle. Next to it I place the Dalai Lama's photograph, and above it I hang a thangka given to me by Rimpoche which shows a refuge tree, in the centre of which is Tsongkhapa. Rimpoche gave me five or six prayers for recitation and I recite these every day. I don't think of myself as a religious person, but I do have so much faith in Rimpoche, and love for him, and I also pray to the Buddha and one or two other figures such as Tārā.

I was always very close to Rimpoche and I used to joke and laugh with him and tell him everything that was on my mind. I was not overawed by him like others were. When I came back from my day at school I would tell Rimpoche whatever had happened and sometimes he would be so amused that he would laugh and laugh. After I married I used to write to Rimpoche three or four times a week. I would sit with Rimpoche whenever I could, and at night I would sleep just outside his room. However much work he had done during the day and however tired he was Rimpoche always finished his prayers before sleeping. Sometimes at one in the morning or later he would adjust my blankets which had fallen off me whilst I was sleeping. I would say to Rimpoche, 'Please sleep. If you don't complete your prayers no one will see you,' and he would just laugh, and of course he would complete his prayers.

Since a very young age and until the time of his death I was closer to Rimpoche than my own parents. It was Rimpoche who chose my husband. This is how it happened: I was quite good at school but at ninth standard I was going through a difficult stage and failed my exams. Rimpoche was very shocked and hurt, but he trusted me, and said that even though I had failed my exams I would become an English teacher at our school. Then he said that I should get married, and he chose my husband, who is the grandson of a lady who at quite an elderly age had become a nun and a disciple of Rimpoche. I had full faith in Rimpoche's choice. After two years I went back to my studies, and passed up to twelfth standard, and now I also have a teacher's certificate and a BA from Calcutta university. Rimpoche expected me to teach at the school, and I definitely plan to, although I am not free to do so yet. I always remember Rimpoche's faith in me and what he expected of me, and I feel I must fulfil that. Rimpoche helped me in so many ways, including giving me money. Whatever was given to Rimpoche was given to him by others out of faith, and since I have benefited from the faith of others I feel I have to live up to that.

In 1994 my second son, Tenzin Legshad, who was born in December 1991, was recognized as the new Dhardo Tulku. When I first heard this I was not happy at all. I just wanted my son to live an ordinary life. Now I have accepted it, but still sometimes it is a cause of worry to me. I see so many Rimpoches in this modern age going for money and luxury goods, and becoming attached to women. Our Rimpoche lived very simply and to me that is how a real Rimpoche should live. He did so much for the refugees, and he had that feeling very early, almost before anyone else. Our Rimpoche always said he must help the poor. Recently I saw a book listing 500 Rimpoches of this century and our Rimpoche was not even listed, which I found very sad.

Yankyidla

Yankyidla was born in 1976 and adopted by Rimpoche when she was two-and-a-half years old.

Rimpoche is everything to me. When I first came to the school I was too young to attend classes and I sat near Rimpoche all day. Rimpoche used to look after me himself and took so much care of me. Later on, when I joined the other hostel children, Rimpoche would come four times a day to hear us recite our prayers before meals. He would stand and listen and then watch us eating our meal, and joke and laugh with us. Every night Rimpoche would come round to where the children were sleeping and spray something under our blankets to prevent us being bitten by fleas.

Whatever I needed I asked Rimpoche for. I was never scared to ask him for anything. If I needed a new pencil I had to ask him, but first I had to show him the end of the old pencil! Later on, when I wanted to go to a movie I asked Rimpoche for the money. Every year at Losar [Tibetan New Year] he would give me a new dress. During construction work at the school Rimpoche would send me to collect any nails that had been bent and thrown on the ground. I would take them to Rimpoche and he would straighten them out and return them to the carpenter. There were many other waste materials that Rimpoche used to collect and I used to help him.

Because of Rimpoche I am not afraid of life. I feel I can face whatever comes. Because of Rimpoche's blessing I never feel something bad will happen to me. Now I feel part of the ITBCI family. I never felt like an orphan. Rimpoche was always playing with us like a family member. We didn't realize then who he was. Now I would give him more respect. When I remember Rimpoche I feel like crying. I don't know how I can ever repay him.

Tsering Wangdi

Tsering Wangdi was born in 1970. He was brought by Rimpoche to the ITBCI School, from Ghoom, at the age of nine.

Every year Rimpoche used to go to the monastery at Ghoom, near Darjeeling, where he was the abbot. I was brought up by my grandmother, who lived near the monastery, and she had recently expired, so on one of these visits, when I was nine years old, Rimpoche took me back to the school. At that time I had never been to school so I had to start in class one. But in this school nobody feels bad if they are older than the others. Now I have completed my studies up to graduation and I have a job as a teacher of Tibetan in Kalimpong.

Rimpoche's determination and his strictness have both been a big influence on me. He taught me how to respect others, and how to lead my life well. Whatever I want to do in life, I think of Rimpoche and the Dalai Lama, and then I make my decision. I especially think of Rimpoche when I am in trouble, or making an important decision, or when I am sick.

Jigmed Wangchug Kaldhen

Jigmed was born in January 1970, the second child of Jampel and Mrs N.C. Kaldhen. Like his elder sister Zenden, he was very close to Rimpoche.

Rimpoche used to tell us that whatever we did, we should do it perfectly, otherwise we shouldn't do it, or we should leave it to him. For example, if we started to unpack a parcel spoiling the paper so that it couldn't be used again, he would take it from us and carefully open it himself. Another example is how he used to manage the pocket money for the hostel children. Parents would leave some rupees with Rimpoche and he would hand out a little money each day. He made a separate envelope for each child, with the money and an account book inside. He would call the children in and sit them in a row, in a precise order which they came to know. And each day he would carefully and neatly make an entry in longhand as to how much he was giving them and the balance remaining. Each child would stand in front of him, and as he gave the coins Rimpoche would always say 'Here's the money,' nothing else, and the child would leave. We used to tell Rimpoche that if he just divided the total money by the days in the term, and handed out the same amount each day, at the end of term there would be nothing left, and this would save his precious time. But he said 'No, the parents have given me this responsibility, and when someone entrusts you with a task you have to give it your best.' So he used to spend twenty or thirty minutes each day in this way.

Rimpoche didn't like to waste anything. For example, if he saw a rubber band outside on the ground he would pick it up saying that whatever you find may come in handy later on. Then later on, when he used it, he would say 'See, I told you it would come in handy.'

What I remember Rimpoche for most of all is his generosity. Rimpoche used to say that if you have one rupee and buy something for yourself, and enjoy it all alone, after five minutes it's gone. If you divide the rupee into two you can share it between two people, and if into four then between four people, and that's a greater happiness. He said that the happiness and peace of mind you get from seeing the happiness of those you have shared with is greater than the happiness of taking for ourselves alone.

When Rimpoche went out he used to carry two money pouches around his waist, one for his own purchases and one for beggars. He always gave more to each beggar than other people, and he never went out without the special pouch. He used to say 'This is very important. If someone is in need of help I can help him in a small way.' Many beggars came directly to the school. In fact they used to come so often, and Rimpoche always gave to them, that we asked them to please come only once a week – and of course on that day Rimpoche gave to them without fail. Whenever walking back from the bazaar Rimpoche always insisted on walking a difficult route, down a very steep slope, because there was a very poor old lady in rags who used to sit there and he wanted to give a rupee to her.

Each week Rimpoche visited a Tibetan women's group at Tenth Mile, and I often accompanied him. At that time his legs were not strong so we used to take a taxi. It cost six rupees, which in those days was quite a lot of money. Rimpoche used to say to me 'Don't tell them I have come by taxi.' I would say, 'Rimpoche, you are going to preach to them, they should give you the money for your fare.' But he would say, 'No, they have called me and it is my duty to go there. How I get there is my problem.'

In order to keep the school going over the years Rimpoche sold many of his possessions. He didn't hesitate and he was never sad. He just said that 'Things come and things go, and by selling these things we can keep the school going.'

The Message of Dhardo Rimpoche

by Sangharakshita

The Message of Dhardo Rimpoche

This is an edited transcript of a talk that Sangharakshita originally gave in 1991, on the first anniversary of Dhardo Rimpoche's death.

I met Dhardo Rimpoche for the first time in 1953, in Kalimpong, the Indian border town in the eastern Himalayas which was already by that time becoming a place of refuge for Tibetan exiles. This was not Dhardo Rimpoche's first encounter with me, however, as I subsequently learned. He had apparently caught sight of me some four years earlier in Bodh Gaya, and had remarked with astonishment on the strange figure of the yellow-robed Western monk, proof that the Dharma gone as far as the West.

My last meeting with Dhardo Rimpoche, also in Kalimpong, was in 1967. Thus I was in personal contact with him for a period of altogether fourteen years. That contact was particularly close, even intense, during the years 1956 to 1964, during which time I received from Rimpoche the Bodhisattva ordination. I naturally, therefore, have very many memories of Rimpoche – memories of his mindfulness, his compassion, and his many other qualities.

But here I am not going to give much in the way of personal reminiscences, or even say much about Rimpoche's life. Instead, I want to say something about what I have come to think of as Dhardo Rimpoche's message. The idea that he had a 'message', other than the powerful message communicated by his life itself, would probably surprise people who knew him. He never wrote any books or gave any lectures in a formal sense. His discourses in Tibetan, some of which I heard, were not recorded or written down, so in a sense they have disappeared.

But although Dhardo Rimpoche didn't write any books or give any lectures, and although his discourses in Tibetan have not been preserved, he did found a school. In

1954 he founded what he always used to call in full the Indo-Tibet Buddhist Cultural Institute School. I remember that he liked very much to pronounce these words – in English – on every possible occasion. He was very proud of his beloved Indo-Tibet Buddhist Cultural Institute School (which, I am glad to say, still exists) and for thirty-six years his life revolved, practically speaking, around it. It was really very dear to him – I can hardly express how dear – and he overcame tremendous obstacles to keep it going. On one occasion he had even to sell some of his precious and beautiful thangkas to pay the wages of his teaching staff.

He didn't love his school as an institution. He didn't love its bricks and stones (or rather its wooden boards – originally it functioned in a big old wooden building). When I say that Rimpoche loved his school, what I mean is that he loved his pupils, thousands of whom must have passed through the school, passed under his care, over the years.

And because Rimpoche loved his pupils so much, he dearly wanted them to grow up under the benign influence of the Dharma. He wanted them to grow up as real Buddhists. That is why the school day began for everybody with the chanting of the praises of the Buddha, as well as the praises of Mañjuśrī, the Bodhisattva of wisdom, and Sarasvatī, the female Bodhisattva of learning and culture, invocation of whom is believed by the Tibetans, as by Indian Buddhists before them, to assist in the preservation of a good memory. That is why the pupils of his school studied – in addition to various modern subjects – the Tibetan language and Tibetan literature. And that is why Rimpoche gave his beloved pupils a message.

But what has this message to do with us? What could a message intended for Tibetan schoolchildren have to say to adults in the very different context of Western culture? Well, it is true that Rimpoche's message was addressed to children. But he saw those children as potential adults and potential Buddhists, even potential Bodhisattvas. He therefore wanted to give them a message that would hold good throughout their lives, a message that they would never forget, a message that would be true wherever they went, whether they returned to Tibet, as many of them hoped they would, or whether they stayed on in India, as very few of them really wanted to do, or whether they even travelled to the West, as some were very anxious to do.

This message, then, is true for all people, especially for all Buddhists – as true for European and American adults as for Tibetan children. After all, we also have a lot to learn, however sophisticated we may consider ourselves to be. We have a lot of spiritual growing up to do.

Dhardo Rimpoche's message is expressed in the motto he gave his school, the motto that is inscribed on the school flag. Although its impact is such that a whole life may be guided by it, it is expressed succinctly. It consists in just seven words in English: 'Cherish the Doctrine, live united, radiate love.'

Cherish the Doctrine

The Doctrine that Rimpoche is asking us to cherish is of course the teaching or doctrine of the Buddha, usually known as the Dharma – the systematic expression in terms of concepts and symbols of the Buddha's experience of the ultimate reality of things, his vision of things as they really are. This expression is of course for our benefit; it is intended to help us realize what the Buddha realized before us. The Buddha himself described it as a raft, a raft which helps us across the stormy waters of saṁsāra to the other shore. But how are we to 'cherish' the Doctrine?

One way of cherishing it is to study it, to study the sūtras and śāstras. The sūtras contain the word of the Buddha, or what tradition regards as such, and the śāstras contain the explanations of the word of the Buddha given by Enlightened masters who lived at a later date. These constitute a vast literature, and we don't of course have to study all of it. In any case, it hasn't all been translated into English. But we should have a thorough knowledge of a reasonable number of key texts – texts which may be of Pāli, Sanskrit, Chinese, or Tibetan origin, since as Western Buddhists we can draw freely from the riches of the entire Buddhist tradition.

In the absence of a knowledge of at least a few such key texts, our thinking about Buddhism will inevitably be muddled and confused, and we may even fall victim to wrong views, something that the Buddhist tradition takes very seriously. Studying the sūtras and śāstras doesn't mean just reading them. It means reflecting on them, turning them over and over in our minds, and discussing them with our teachers and our fellow students.

We also cherish the Doctrine by practising it. (Of course, we can only practise it if we have at least some knowledge of it.) We practise the Doctrine by Going for Refuge to the Buddha, Dharma, and Sangha, and by trying continually to deepen that Going for Refuge. We practise the Doctrine by observing the precepts – five, or ten, or more. We practise it by engaging in Right Livelihood. We practise it by cultivating spiritual friendship, the supreme importance of which the Buddhist tradition continually emphasizes. We practise it by meditating and performing puja. We practise it by living in spiritual communities. We practise it by helping to run Buddhist centres. We practise it by going on solitary retreat. In all these, and a hundred other ways, we practise – we can practise, we should practise – the Dharma. And to the extent that we practise it, we cherish it, we help to keep it alive.

It is not easy to practise the Dharma, as anyone who has tried to do it knows. Practising the Dharma means going against the stream, ultimately going against the whole weight of our mundane conditioning. But if we don't practise the Dharma, it will not be cherished; and if it is not cherished, it won't really live, and we shall have in its place only ideas, concepts, words.

Thirdly, we cherish the Doctrine by propagating it. Obviously we can do this only to the extent that we understand it and practise it, only if we experience it and realize it ourselves. There are many ways in which we can propagate the Dharma. We can literally teach it, by giving lectures or leading meditation classes, or by writing books. But not everybody is in a position to do this. Most people help propagate the Dharma more indirectly, and this can be done in many ways – by transcribing and editing the tapes of lectures, for example, or by publishing books, or by providing facilities for the giving of lectures and the organizing of classes, or by donating money.

It goes without saying that people in the world today need the Dharma. Many of them know that they need it, but they don't always know that what they need is what Buddhists call the Dharma – hence their surprise and delight when they happen to come at last in contact with it, perhaps after many years of searching. This is sometimes quite an overwhelming experience. The letters I receive from people who have recently made contact with Buddhism, in many different parts of the world, invariably express relief, joy, thankfulness, and gratitude.

We should therefore do all we can to propagate the Dharma in every possible way. If we propagate the Dharma, people will come to know and understand it. If they understand it, they will be able to practise it. If they practise it, they will cherish it too. And if it is cherished, it will survive. Nowadays there are many obstacles to the survival of the Dharma. It is, in fact, threatened on every side – by materialism, for example, and by pseudo-religious fundamentalism. It therefore needs to be propagated more vigorously than ever.

But – and this is very important – it is the Dharma and only the Dharma that must be propagated. We mustn't mix the Dharma with isms and ologies that are quite foreign to its spirit, even quite inimical to it. In our work of propagating the Dharma we need to use traditional Buddhist language as far as possible. The message of the Buddha cannot be delivered in the language of Māra – or in one of his languages, for he has many – not even by Bodhisattvas. (At the same time we have to admit that Māra himself can on occasion use, or appear to use, the language of Buddhism. But that is another story.)

So we should cherish the Doctrine: by studying it, by practising it, and by propagating it.

Live united

This is the second aspect of Dhardo Rimpoche's message. And, obviously, people do live united in a sense. Without unity social life would be impossible. But what kind of unity is this? It has a number of underlying factors – language, nationality or citizenship, race, culture, religion: all these factors bind certain groups of people together.

But when Rimpoche exhorts us to live united, it is not this kind of unity he has in mind. We are already living united – more or less – in that mundane way. We are already bound to other people by language, nationality, and so on; we don't need any exhortation in this respect. Rimpoche clearly has a different kind of unity in mind. We mustn't forget that exhortation is addressed to potential real Buddhists. And the unifying factors in our collective existence, the factors that bind us together as Buddhists, are, obviously, the Three Jewels. We are united primarily by virtue of the fact that we all go for Refuge to the Buddha, the Dharma, and the Sangha. We observe the same precepts, practise the same meditations, perform the same pujas, study the same texts, and so on. These are the things that in principle unite us.

But do we in fact live united? Do we put that unity into practice? Is it effective in our actual relations with one another? That is only too often another matter. When Dhardo Rimpoche says 'Live united,' he is saying, 'You are united as Buddhists in principle, but you must also be united in practice.'

What prevents us from living united in practice? What prevents us from being a spiritual community in the fullest sense? I am afraid there are quite a number of things. There is personal conflict – that is to say, conflict with other members of the spiritual community. And there are many other factors: competitiveness, jealousy, factionalism, the cherishing of ill will, the harbouring of grudges, unwillingness to forgive, reluctance to clear up misunderstandings. All these things prevent us as a spiritual community from living united, prevent us from putting into practice the unity in which we believe in principle.

What prevents us from living united is, in a word, egotism – or, if that word is unacceptably old-fashioned, individualism. Only too often we think that we are acting as individuals when we are really only being individualistic. When Rimpoche says, 'Live united,' he is also saying, in a deeper sense, 'Live egolessly. Live in a non-individualistic manner. Realize that there is in the ultimate sense no separate unchanging self to defend or to assert. Realize *nairātmyatā*, realize *śūnyatā*.'

Radiate love

This brings us to the third and last part of Rimpoche's message: radiate love. The English word love is dreadfully ambiguous. It can mean lust in the sense of sexual craving, as when we speak of making love. It can mean a sort of greedy liking, as when someone says, 'Oh, I love chocolate.' It can also mean natural affection, as when we speak of a mother's love for her child, or of brotherly love. Then there's love in the sense of romantic infatuation, which can also be called projected love, because it involves the projection on to the loved person of qualities that he or she does not possess, or not to the degree that the lover thinks they do. This is what we call, in case you haven't tumbled it, 'being in love'. Finally there is altruistic or sacrificial love. We don't have an adequate word for this in English, although the Authorized Version of the Bible refers to it when it says, 'Greater love hath no man than this, that he lay down his life for his friend.' It is important to distinguish the different meanings of the word love, otherwise there will be confusion in our thinking and probably confusion in our personal life as well.

When Rimpoche says 'Radiate love,' he means radiate *mettā*, or *mettā* and *karuṇā*. *Karuṇā* means compassion, and the Pāli word *mettā* is cognate with *mitta* (*mitra* in Sanskrit), which means simply 'friend'. Mettā is thus the intense, non-sexual, altruistic, delighted affection that you feel for a friend. It is love in this sense that Rimpoche is asking us to radiate. In other words we need to radiate friendliness, to develop an attitude of spiritual friendship.

The importance of friendship, especially spiritual friendship, constitutes one of the cornerstones of the Buddhist movement I founded, the Friends of the Western Buddhist Order, and we do make an effort to practise it, to be real friends, true friends, good friends, to one another. But, of course, our practice of friendship is far from perfect. It

is not easy to be a real friend; there are so many obstacles to friendship, especially deep friendship, perhaps now more than ever.

Friendship is deep, one could say, to the extent to which it incorporates the transcendental, or rather to the extent that it is incorporated in the transcendental. It is deep to the extent that it is altruistic. It is deep to the extent that it is egoless. Deep friendship can be thought of as mutual awareness leading to mutual self-transcendence. Thus, true friendship, one could say, is the efflorescence of egolessness. In other words, we can radiate love only to the extent that we live united.

To radiate means, according to the dictionary, 'to emit from a centre'. The centre is the middle point – and a point is defined as that which has position without magnitude. The choice of this word is therefore very meaningful. We can radiate love only from the middle point of our being, from egolessness, from *śūnyatā* – from that point within ourselves which has position without magnitude.

'Cherish the Doctrine, live united, radiate love.' This is the message that Dhardo Rimpoche gave to his students, and to each one of us. He gave it not just in words but in deeds, through the medium of his own life. He himself did indeed cherish the Doctrine. It was very dear to him and he studied it intensively, especially during the earlier part of his life. He practised it as well, observing the ethics of a Bodhisattva, cultivating the pāramitās, and, for practically seventy years, living the life of a monk. And he propagated the Doctrine, especially towards the end of his life. As well as teaching the students of his own school, he cooperated with visiting Buddhist scholars and practitioners, especially those from the West, and he gave advice and inspiration to visiting members and friends of the Western Buddhist Order.

Indeed, he once said that he regarded my disciples as his own. He could say this because he himself lived united. He was free, totally free, from competitiveness and jealousy. On more than one occasion, as I saw myself during my time in Kalimpong, he had to suffer, really suffer, at the hands of bigots. But he didn't bear a grudge. He was always willing to forgive. And he could do this because he was not the victim of egotism.

And he radiated love, compassion, and friendliness. All those who came in contact with him, even for a short time, experienced this for themselves. He was the embodiment of his own message. He himself cherished the Doctrine, he lived united, and he radiated love. This is why we are celebrating the anniversary of Rimpoche's death: because of the supreme quality of his life. We are celebrating the anniversary of his death because his life is worth remembering, worth bearing in mind, reflecting upon, and gaining inspiration from. We are celebrating the anniversary of his death because we want to make his life a permanent part of the heritage of the FWBO.

CHERISH THE DOCTRINE

LIVE UNITED RADIATE LOVE

The Flag

Dhardo Rimpoche designed a flag for his school, and wrote the following description for the 1963 School Report.

On the page opposite is the school flag, and as with all Tibetan designs it is not merely decorative but illustrates a number of aspects of the Dharma, so it is hoped that this short note of interpretation will be of some help.

The design of the pennant within the circle is very ancient, being described in the *Vinaya Sūtra* of the Sarvāstivādins as a proper emblem to fly above a vihara. Its three turnings indicated the triple training (*triśikṣā*) of the Buddha's teaching: morality, meditation, and wisdom. Superimposed on this ancient banner are the three chimeric animals: an eagle-lion, a fish-otter, and a crocodile-conch, the meaning of which is given in the legend that when Śākyamuni found Enlightenment at Bodh Gaya, all enemies amongst men and animals came together to live in peace, thus producing these hybrids. Here, pairs of animals traditionally in conflict with each other are shown united, like a harmony of opposing forces.

This jewel-like pennant is painted on an orange sun radiating in a deep blue sky. Here is expressed another teaching of the Buddha: that loving-kindness (*maitrī*) should be so cultivated that it becomes a powerful, indeed universal, radiation.

Above the sun are the Three Jewels – the Buddha, Dharma, and Sangha – and above them the trikāya or three 'bodies' of the Buddha: the moon shining by reflected light is the nirmānakāya, the appearance body seen here by men and animals; the sun blazing splendidly forth is the sambhogakāya, the glorified body perceived in concentrated meditations and by spiritual beings; while the vajra represents the dharmakāya, or Immutable Truth.

Below the sun of maitrī is the dharmacakra, the wheel of the Dharma first turned by Śākyamuni's teaching in the Deer Park at Sarnath. The eight spokes of the wheel represent the Noble Eightfold Path taught there by the Buddha as his practical way to spiritual attainment. He also taught the Four Noble Truths, seen here as the four jewels that surround the wheel. To symbolize that all this teaching derives from his Enlightenment, there are three divisions at the centre of the wheel, again illustrating the trikāya doctrine. All this is supported by a lotus frame, illustrating the Dharma's sublime nature, from the ends of which rise lotuses growing aloft: the Dharma is in the world but not of the world, growing from the mud but, being transcendental, unstained by it.

In this explanation are found the three elements of the motto inscribed at the bottom: 'Cherish the Doctrine' is shown in the way and the wheel, the triratna, and the trikāya, 'Live united' is seen in the three strange animals, while 'Radiate love' is expressed by the symbol of the sun in the void.

With such a glorious flag, so deep in meaning, may all this school go forward indeed to CHERISH THE DOCTRINE, LIVE UNITED, RADIATE LOVE!

Rejoicing in Merit

Composed by Sangharakshita

I rejoice in the merits
Of the Guru of Dhartsendo;
I rejoice in his life
Of mindfulness and compassion.
I rejoice in his confident turning
Of the Wheel of the Immaculate Dharma,
And in his fautless wielding
Of the Diamond Sceptre of Wisdom.
I rejoice in his proclamation
To his disciples both young and old,
To his disciples both near and far,
Of the threefold inspiring message
To cherish the Doctrine, live united, and radiate love.
I rejoice in his practice
Of the six perfections:
In his practice of unfailing Generosity;
In his practice of flawless Ethics and Manners;
In his practice of infinite Forbearance;
In his practice of inexhaustible Vigour;
In his practice of unshakeable Concentration;
In his practice of profound and far-reaching Wisdom.

Humbly and heartily,
Gratefully and reverentially,
With body, speech, and mind,
I rejoice in the merits
Of the Guru of Dhartsendo,
I rejoice in the merits
Of Dhardo Rimpoche.

Further Reading

FOR MORE ABOUT DHARDO RIMPOCHE

Suvajra, *The Wheel and the Diamond*, Windhorse, Glasgow 1991. A comprehensive biography of Dhardo Rimpoche.

FOR MORE ABOUT SANGHARAKSHITA

Sangharakshita, *The Rainbow Road*, Windhorse, Birmingham 1997.
Sangharakshita, *Facing Mount Kanchenjunga*, Windhorse, Glasgow 1991.
Sangharakshita, *In the Sign of the Golden Wheel*, Windhorse, Birmingham 1996.
These engaging volumes of memoirs recount Sangharakshita's unique experiences as an English Buddhist monk in India in the 1950s.

FOR MORE ABOUT TIBETAN BUDDHISM

Sangharakshita, *Tibetan Buddhism: An Introduction*, Windhorse, Birmingham 1996.
Lama Anagarika Govinda, *The Way of the White Clouds*, Rider, London 1992. A classic tale of pilgrimage through Tibet and Govinda's insights into the Tibetan tradition.
Matthieu Ricard, *Journey to Enlightenment*, Aperture Foundation, New York 1996. A beautiful portrayal of another of Sangharakshita's eight main teachers, Dilgo Khyentse Rimpoche.

FOR MORE ON THE BODHISATTVA IDEAL AND ARCHETYPAL BODHISATTVAS

Sangharakshita, *The Bodhisattva Ideal*, Windhorse, Birmingham 1999. An exploration of the Bodhisattva ideal, one of the sublimest spiritual ideals mankind has ever seen.
Vessantara, *Meeting the Buddhas*, Windhorse, Birmingham 1993. A vivid and informed introduction to the magical realm of the Buddhas, Bodhisattvas, and wrathful deities of the Buddhist tantric tradition.
Marylin M. Rhie and Robert F. Thurman, *The Sacred Art of Tibet,* Thames and Hudson, London 1996. A beautiful, highly-illustrated book that looks at Tibetan Buddhist art in terms of its religious meaning, purpose, and function.

The Karuna Trust

The ITBCI School in Kalimpong, which Dhardo Rimpoche founded, continues to provide an education for children from the Tibetan refugee community. The school now provides places for more than 200 children and continues to place great emphasis on the preservation of traditional Tibetan culture.

Most of the school's running costs are met by the Karuna Trust, a Western Buddhist charity that exists to support educational and health projects among poor Buddhist communities in India. Karuna relies for its work on donations from members of the public.

If you would like to find out more about Karuna, or make a donation towards the running of Dhardo Rimpoche's school, please write to:

THE KARUNA TRUST
ST MARK'S STUDIOS
CHILLINGWORTH ROAD
LONDON
N7 8QJ
UK

Windhorse Publications

The Windhorse symbolizes the energy of the enlightened mind carrying the Three Jewels – the Buddha, the Dharma, and the Sangha – to all sentient beings.

Buddhism is one of the fastest growing spiritual traditions in the Western world. Throughout its 2,500-year history, it has always succeeded in adapting its mode of expression to suit whatever culture it has encountered.

Windhorse Publications aims to continue this tradition as Buddhism comes to the West. Today's Westerners are heirs to the entire Buddhist tradition, free to draw instruction and inspiration from all the many schools and branches. Windhorse publishes works by authors who not only understand the Buddhist tradition but are also familiar with Western culture and the Western mind.

For orders and catalogues contact

WINDHORSE PUBLICATIONS
11 PARK ROAD
BIRMINGHAM
B13 8AB
UK

WINDHORSE BOOKS
PO BOX 574
NEWTOWN
NSW 2042
AUSTRALIA

WEATHERHILL INC
41 MONROE TUNRPIKE
TRUMBULL
CT 06611
USA

The Friends of the Western Buddhist Order

Windhorse Publications is an arm of the Friends of the Western Buddhist Order, which has more than sixty centres on five continents. Through these centres, members of the Western Buddhist Order offer regular programmes of events for the general public and for more experienced students. These include meditation classes, public talks, study on Buddhist themes and texts, and 'bodywork' classes such as t'ai chi, yoga, and massage. The FWBO also runs several retreat centres and the Karuna Trust, a fund-raising charity that supports social welfare projects in the slums and villages of India.

Many FWBO centres have residential spiritual communities and ethical businesses associated with them. Arts activities are encouraged too, as is the development of strong bonds of friendship between people who share the same ideals. In this way the FWBO is developing a unique approach to Buddhism, not simply as a set of techniques, less still as an exotic cultural interest, but as a creatively directed way of life for people living in the modern world.

If you would like more information about the FWBO visit the website at www.fwbo.org or write to

LONDON BUDDHIST CENTRE
51 ROMAN ROAD
LONDON
E2 0HU
UK

ARYALOKA
HEARTWOOD CIRCLE
NEWMARKET
NEW HAMPSHIRE
NH 03857
USA

If you don't know what to do, do something for others